THEORY BUILDING IN SOCIAL WORK

THE HARRY M. CASSIDY
MEMORIAL RESEARCH FUND

The Cassidy Memorial Research Fund was established in 1952 to commemorate the pioneer work of the late Harry M. Cassidy, Director of the School of Social Work, University of Toronto, 1945-1951. In particular it is intended to further Harry Cassidy's conviction that the policies of social welfare and practices of social work need to be based on objective study and research. It is an essential principle of research that the results should be published and available for study and use. For this reason the Fund sponsors publication of the results of research work when it is satisfied that the work has been thoroughly done and the material is of intrinsic value. Publication under the sponsorship of the Fund does not imply responsibility for the content of the work, or agreement with the opinions expressed: these are properly the responsibility of the authors.

THEORY BUILDING

IN SOCIAL WORK

Gordon Hearn

CASSIDY RESEARCH VISITING PROFESSOR 1955-1956
UNIVERSITY OF TORONTO
ASSOCIATE PROFESSOR, SCHOOL OF SOCIAL WELFARE
UNIVERSITY OF CALIFORNIA, BERKELEY

UNIVERSITY OF TORONTO PRESS: 1958

PREFACE

This is essentially a book *about* theory building. Instead of actually presenting theory, it suggests and illustrates a particular way in which the social work profession, or any of the other service professions, might pursue the task of developing theory to refine its mode of practice. While written for every professional, it is directed, in particular, to those most actively engaged in the development and refinement of theory for their profession. It is a personal document in the sense that it is a chronicle of the author's reflections about how a profession might pursue most profitably this aspect of its total function.

The record of such reflective enterprises often suggests a greater degree of orderliness, when finished, than actually characterized its process of development. Certainly, such is the case of this present undertaking, for there was much circuitous exploration and groping, and there were many fresh beginnings before it assumed its final form. As an example, the three chapters on theory building, which constitute Part I, were written, indeed they could only have been written, *after* the author had had the experience of encountering and developing the material presented in Part II.

Focus of Study

The focus of the project changed several times. Initially, it was intended to try to develop a framework within which to describe the role of the social group worker, in the belief that if the newer concepts and methodology of the behavioural sciences could be applied to the task, a fuller understanding of the social group worker's role might be achieved.

This was soon abandoned, however, in favour of a similar but broader focus on the role of the social worker, occasioned, undoubtedly, by a growing conviction that there is a function or role common to all social workers regardless of whether they work primarily with individuals, groups, or communities. Thus the focus changed to that of developing a conceptual framework within which to represent the role of the *social worker*.

As might have been expected, when the dimensions of this task were examined more closely, it became abundantly clear that it would be a very large and complex undertaking. Consequently the various parts of the larger task were examined in order to select an appropriate place to begin. It was decided that as an initial step it would be useful to try to develop a way of conceiving and representing the objective realities—the clients—with which the social worker deals. The widely supported contention that social workers deal primarily with individuals, groups, and communities was accepted as valid. But since the objective, now, was to contribute to the ultimate development of a unified conception of the social worker's role, a way was sought of representing clients as part of an integrated complex consisting of individuals—in groups—in communities. This latter objective was to become the ultimate, though not the immediate, focus of the project.

At this stage, and by what can only be described as a fortunate accident, recent publications of the general systems theorists[1] were encountered. These scientists were contending that all forms of animate matter, including individuals, groups, and communities, together with various forms of inanimate matter could be regarded as systems; that, as such, they had certain common properties; and that eventually the laws governing their functioning would be known. If this were so, it seemed to be closely related to, and to hold great promise for, what was being attempted in the present project.

As general systems theory was explored more intensively, study and reading moved more and more into the fields of biology, chemistry, and physics and into the philosophy and methodology of science until, eventually, the focus of the project shifted once more, and for the last time, to a concern about the process of building theory in a profession.

Thus, the objective of this phase of the larger project finally became that of describing one way of developing theory in a profession such as social work, illustrating it, as far as possible, by the experience gained in the various phases of the exploration.

METHOD OF WORK

While this is the chronicle of a personal experience, it is in another sense a group product in that it represents one person's interpretations of the ideas of a great many others contributing through him to the project.

What is reported here is the work that has been accomplished in the first two years of the project. Beginning at the School of Social Work, University of Toronto, while the author occupied the position of Cassidy Research Visiting Professor, it has been continued in the second year by a research group[2] under his direction at the School of Social Welfare, University of California, Berkeley.

During the year at Toronto a very sketchy formulation was completed after about six weeks and presented to an audience of social work educators and practitioners. This formulation led, after a number of individual consultations and further reading, to a second, which was distributed to, or discussed with, social work educators, researchers, and practitioners and with selected social scientists thought to have a special interest in such a project. Many of these persons laboured long to give their critical comments and suggestions and these, together with further personal research, led to a written report of the Toronto phase of the work.[3]

[1] James G. Miller, "Toward a General Theory for the Behavioral Sciences," *American Psychologist*, 10 (1955), pp. 513-531.

[2] The Berkeley research group consisted of Virginia Carlson, Henrietta Gillenwater, Jackye Hutchins, Wanda R. McNeill, Helen Perroti, Roberta Solbrig, and Ann Tompkins.

[3] Gordon Hearn, "Toward Theory Building in Social Work" (unpublished report on file in the School of Social Work, University of Toronto, Toronto, 1956).

Working this way was hazardous. It meant that one had to expose one's ideas to critical scrutiny while they were still very crudely and partially conceived. It meant, too, that just as one had achieved a tidy arrangement of one's ideas, some correspondent might suggest a new idea which necessitated a substantial revision. This happened several times during the development of the present formulation. Despite the hazards, however, such a procedure could be and was a most stimulating and rewarding experience.

The Berkeley group began its work with a thorough examination and assimilation of the Toronto report. Accepting the contention stressed therein that a researcher ought to make explicit at the outset the philosophical base from which he approaches his theory domain, the Berkeley group searched and shared their own beliefs and finally formulated a statement concerning the nature of human beings and their destiny. They formulated, as well, their position concerning the process of knowing, because this they knew was a central consideration in the theory building process. With this as a background they addressed themselves to two research questions:

1. Can the clients with whom social workers are concerned in practice be described in terms of general systems theory?
2. When so described, does such translation lead to useful insights for practice?

In quest of answers, and using a general systems framework, four of the members attempted to describe, respectively, an individual client, a client group, a social work agency, and the social work profession. Another attempted to integrate Freud's conception of the psyche into the general systems framework. The remaining two group members dealt with certain matters concerning the strategy of theory building.

This book, then, is primarily a report of the work done in Toronto but reflects, as well, the subsequent influence and the substantial contributions of the Berkeley group.[4]

ACKNOWLEDGEMENTS

Only rarely in the course of a professional career is a person released, even temporarily, from the responsibilities of his regular work and afforded a period for unhurried reflection and creative enterprise. In one sense it is a tremendous relief to be thus freed from the unrelenting and exacting demands of teaching, administration and professional service, free to pursue one's own interests and curiosities. But in another sense it is very demanding, for one feels compelled to exploit to the maximum an opportunity so infrequently granted.

Viewing the Toronto year in retrospect, the author experiences a mixture of feelings. Above all, there is a sense of honour in having served in the name of so great a social statesman as Harry M. Cassidy, and gratitude to those who, in his memory, have made such an experience possible, who through their hospi-

[4] For a full report of the work of the Berkeley Group see V. Carlson *et al.*, "Social Work and General Systems Theory" (unpublished group research report, School of Social Welfare, University of California, Berkeley, 1957).

tality and kindness made it so pleasant, and through their substantive contributions made it so rewarding a year. At the same time, there is some feeling of frustation as one recalls numerous instances of having failed to take full advantage of the opportunities that were offered.

There are many to whom one wishes to acknowledge a special debt of gratitude. There is the University of Toronto, whose resources, and particularly its magnificent library, proved more than adequate for the present undertaking. There is the School of Social Work, its faculty and director, Charles E. Hendry, whose interest is most gratefully acknowledged. The faculty showed unusual forbearance and tolerance when the author's enthusiasm for what the School was doing often tempted him to transgress the bounds of involvement appropriate to a *visiting* professor. One is grateful also to the Award Committee of the Harry M. Cassidy Memorial Research Fund, for the generous provisions of the Research Visiting Professorship; the members of the Advisory Faculty Committee of the Fund, for their encouragement, their patience and their sound guidance in the conception and development of the project. One remembers, particularly, numerous colleagues in the social work profession and the social sciences whose critical evaluations of the formulation in its various stages of development were so very helpful. And there are the members of the 1957 Berkeley Research Group whose important refinements are reflected at so many points in the substance of this report. To all, a most sincere expression of appreciation.

Finally, a very special word of thanks to Mrs. Florence C. Strakhovsky, Secretary of the Fund. Her industry, persistence and patience were unbounded. Her secretarial skills and editorial assistance were of inestimable value as the author struggled to understand and then to express in communicable form the many new and abstruse concepts he was encountering in his explorations of general systems theory.

G. H.

Berkeley, California
September, 1957

CONTENTS

Part I

THE THEORY BUILDING PROCESS

Chapter I

PROFESSIONAL PRACTICE AND THE
PURSUIT OF KNOWLEDGE

Practice is professional to the extent that it is sanctioned by society. Such sanction to practise and to educate for practice is earned as a field demonstrates its ability to perform its prescribed functions with integrity, knowledge, and skill. To act with professional integrity is to act consistently within a framework of values that is shared generally by the members of the profession. To act with knowledge is to act with an awareness of the rationale and probable consequences of one's actions. To act with skill is to exercise such control that one's actions more closely approximate one's intentions. Thus, professional practice is a combination of believing, knowing, and doing.

Professions exist primarily to promote these three processes. It is a function of a profession continually to define and redefine the value assumptions upon which practice is based. It is a function of a profession to extend knowledge so that its members may increase their understanding of what they are doing and how it should be done. It is a function of a profession to help its members to acquire an acceptable level of skill and then progressively to extend that skill.

While this discussion is concerned necessarily with all three functions of believing, knowing, and doing, since each is a part of an indivisible whole, it focuses primarily upon the second process—the efforts in the profession to extend knowledge. How does knowledge engage and enrich professional practice? How, ideally, might this knowing process be pursued within the social work profession? How might the members of the profession most effectively participate in the process?

Elements in the Knowing Process

It is important at the outset to realize that when we speak here of the knowing process we refer to something far more extensive than the traditional scientific method. There are many methods of knowing, of which scientific knowing is a particular kind. It is a step-by-step process moving from the realization of the existence of an obscure situation needing clarification through the successive steps of stating the problem in specific terms, formulating a working hypothesis, devising a controlled method of investigation, gathering data, translating data into statements having meaning and significance, arriving at an assertion which seems warranted, and finally integrating the new knowledge with the body of knowledge already established.

But such scientific knowing does not exhaust all possible ways of knowing the world. There is, for example, a common sense and pragmatic way of acquiring knowledge which can hardly be characterized as scientific. As a child grows up he learns a tremendous amount about his world, but the method whereby he acquires his understanding is certainly not scientific. Anyone who reads the history of science will be impressed by the fact that here, too, certain other kinds of activities in combination with the scientific method have also extended knowledge.

Ernest Greenwood[1] has suggested that a great portion of knowledge in the field of social work has been achieved in a manner other than scientific. Social workers have acquired much of what they know pragmatically and impressionistically. The task before us, he believes, is to subject to scientific test the social work knowledge that has been acquired non-scientifically. The question is: how much of that knowledge will survive the test of the scientific method?

First we need to understand the dimensions of the knowing process in general, to which end a logical first step would seem to be that of identifying and describing the elements which constitute this general knowing process. Each element, as we shall see, is a somewhat different kind of activity.

The first might best be described as *experiencing* in which one observes and acts almost intuitively. As an illustration, James B. Conant[2] cites the labours of an excellent cook. Despite all our knowledge of the chemistry of proteins, fats, carbohydrates, he says, the recipe for a good sauce or a good dessert is still entirely empirical. A part of social work practice may be of the same order. There are individual practitioners who are unusually effective in helping clients but who apparently do so intuitively and with little sense of why they do what they do. They know the conditions without knowing the reasons that lead to success. This is not to imply that such activity is unimportant. On the contrary, we would hold, as does Conant, that pure empiricism is an indispensable element in the knowing process, for it provides the raw data out of which understanding ultimately emerges. It is, however, the function of the scientific process to reduce the extent to which the practitioner must rely upon pure intuition as the basis for practical decisions.

A second type of activity might be described as *well-ordered empirical inquiry*. This may be illustrated by reference to any one of a number of social problems such as alcoholism, juvenile delinquency, homicide or suicide. Empirical inquiry, conducted according to the most rigorous application of the scientific method, may be instituted in an effort to establish their causes, as a preliminary step toward their ultimate control. Such inquiry may establish a relationship between delinquency, for instance, and factors such as intelligence, disruption within the home, or ethnic and socio-economic background. It may suggest that delinquency is related in some way to the sex factor, since its incidence is higher among boys than girls, or that it is related to the maturation process, since its incidence is higher at certain periods in the life cycle than at others.

[1] Comments made by Ernest Greenwood in discussion of a paper "Theory Building in a Profession" (read by the author before the Faculty Colloquium, School of Social Welfare, University of California, Berkeley, 1956).

[2] James B. Conant, *Modern Science and Modern Man* (New York: Columbia University Press, 1952), p. 43.

All of this is useful information, for it contributes to our understanding of the problem and enables us to move, to some extent at least, toward developing programmes for its control. On the basis of such information we may, for instance, replace the slums with public housing; we may strive to be more understanding and vigilant in our work with boys, particularly adolescent boys, and witness some decrease in delinquency.

While well-ordered empirical inquiry of this nature is an essential element, it is limited in the extent to which it can lead to a full understanding of the problem. It can tell us the conditions under which delinquency occurs but it may not always be able to tell us the basic cause or causes. It can tell us where we are likely to find a high incidence of delinquency but it cannot, or at least it usually has not, told us why certain individuals living under such conditions do, while others do not, become delinquent. A fuller understanding seems to require a third kind of activity. Conant says that this other activity consists of the use of new concepts, new conceptual schemes that serve as working hypotheses on a grand scale,[3] perhaps most appropriately called *conceptualizing*.

An excellent example of it, although derived from the field of chemistry, is the story of the brewery industry's long struggle to master the brewing process. It illustrates at different stages the three levels of activities that we have described. For a long time there were brew masters who could mix ingredients and produce excellent beer without ever knowing the chemical formula of what they produced or the chemical processes involved. At this stage the industry was plagued by the fact that at times, for unexplained reasons, beer would become acid or rotten and disastrous losses would result. They conducted well-ordered empirical inquiry and discovered the conditions under which deterioration occurred, but since they did not establish the cause, they could not completely overcome the problem which kept arising under new conditions. Little progress was made until Louis Pasteur postulated an important new hypothesis. According to an early account by John Tyndall,[4] Pasteur had shown that living micro-organisms were the "hidden enemies" with which the brewer had contended without knowing it. On the basis of this knowledge, Pasteur postulated the bold working hypothesis that fermentation and putrefaction were the consequences of the growth of micro-organisms. Once this step had been taken, means were soon found to overcome the problems of acidity and rottenness.

In the realm of social work, one can cite the work of Perlman *et al.*[5] in Chicago as another example of conceptualizing of the type herein described. It is their hypothesis that casework is essentially a process of solving problems and that the ego is the prime agent in the process. Diagnosis, as they see it, consists of determining the client's motivation, capacity, and opportunity to solve a particular problem. The value of such a view of the casework process, they believe,

---

[3] *Ibid.*, p. 46.

[4] Published in *Essays on the Floating-Matter of the Air in Relation to Putrefaction and Infection* (London: Longmans and Co., 1881).

[5] For a discussion of casework as a process of solving problems see H. H. Perlman, "The Basic Structure of the Case-work Process," *Social Service Review*, 27 (1953), pp. 308-315, and L. Ripple, "Motivation, Capacity and Opportunity as Related to the Use of Casework Service: Plan of Study," *Social Service Review*, 29 (1955), pp. 172-193.

is that it permits one to focus more directly upon an immediate problem. One does not have to do a total personality diagnosis in order to deal with the immediate presenting problem.

In the field of social welfare, there is perhaps no hypothesis, conceived on a grand scale, to surpass Freud's revolutionary contention that much of behaviour is motivated by unconscious impulses and that an essential step toward the control of such behaviour is to help the individual to bring these hidden impulses to the level of consciousness. The "discovery" of the unconscious broke a log-jam in the stream of progress which has led to a whole new series of empirical inquiries and a vast extension of our understanding of human behaviour. This process of conceptualization is discussed further in the next chapter; indeed, the entire second part of this book is a description of one attempt to engage in such activity.

A fourth type of scientific activity is *testing* or verifying theories. Theorizing as such does not lead inevitably to greater understanding. There are good and bad theories, some which lead toward understanding, some which lead nowhere at all, or at best to confusion. Even among the good theories, some are better than others in the sense that they are able to "explain" a greater number of observed phenomena. Theory testing, consequently, is an indispensable part of the pursuit of knowledge.

Testing may take any one or more of several forms. It may be logical, experimental, or empirical. One may specify all the ramifications that flow logically from a central concept, such as the concept of the unconscious, for instance, and then consider whether the derivative postulates are consistent with the facts as one knows them. This might be regarded, perhaps, as "arm-chair" verification. And it may be sufficient to lead one to accept a central concept, to abandon it, or to retain it pending further verification.

Once one has defined the derivative hypotheses which follow from a central hypothesis, one may then institute a programme of research to put the various hypotheses to their crucial test. Such experimentation may be done "in the field" or it may be done under the less "real" but more controlled situation of a laboratory. Ideally, a research programme moves back and forth between the field and the laboratory, thereby capitalizing on the unique values of both. Perhaps the crucial test of a theory is whether or not it helps the practitioner to understand more fully what he is doing and subsequently to practise more effectively. This is the empirical test.

The fifth type of activity or element in the knowing process is what we choose to call, for want of a better term, *concretizing*. Its necessity derives from the fact that the ordering and conceptualizing of experience can be conducted only in the language of abstraction. Ordering and conceptualizing represent successively higher levels of abstraction. Consequently, before a theory that is developed out of conceptualization can be applied in practice it must be retranslated, so to speak, into the language of practice. A recently published book[6] may serve to illustrate the nature and function of this activity. The

---

[6] Alan F. Klein, *Role Playing* (New York: Association Press, 1956).

publishers describe the book as "a manual, an easily-understood, step-by-step guide which gives you the Why, When and How of using role-playing to develop leadership abilities and seek solutions to questions that concern your group." The engineer's field manual could be cited as another example of this concretizing function.

Manuals are usually based on theory, although rarely do they make the underlying theory explicit. They translate it into the practical operation which the theory prescribes. The contribution of such concretizing to the scientific process is that it enables theory to be put more completely and more quickly to the empirical test. And further, to the extent that it thus enables theory to enrich practice, it thereby produces a new order of practical experience out of which still greater understanding can emerge.

A sixth activity which can be regarded as an element in the scientific process is *communication*. While it is a type of activity in its own right, it should perhaps be regarded as somewhat different from those already discussed. It serves as an important means by which the other activities are accomplished. It may be worth noting that communication necessarily takes different forms in relation to the other activities in the knowing process. Experiences, for instance, can be communicated among people, to some extent, through the non-verbal language of action. Empirical inquiry, however, requires a greater use of descriptive symbols, and conceptualizing often requires the use of the language of mathematics and logic. Concretizing, as has already been suggested, is actually a process of translating from the language of theory into the language of action. The language of practice alone cannot be used in theory building, nor can that of theory be used in practice, as anyone who has tried either will attest.

Effective communication depends, too, upon the availability of specialized channels or media of communication appropriate to the particular function of each type of activity in the knowing process. We often deplore the variety and number of media used to transmit the spoken word and we despair at the proliferation of journals and books required to communicate the written word; we wonder if all are necessary. Perhaps they are not, although their number and variety can partly be justified by the fact that specialized media are required to communicate different kinds of material.

The Knowing Process as a Functional Unity

The several elements in the knowing process have been discussed separately here only for the sake of clearer exposition and not to convey the impression that they function independently, for such is not the case. The fact is that the several activities which constitute the knowing process function as an interdependent whole.

In order fully to understand the manner in which they thus function as a dynamic whole it is necessary to understand an additional characteristic of all of the activities that have been identified as constituents of the knowing process. Each functions as a circular process. The activity we have called experiencing, for example, can thus be regarded as a circular process in that it seems to

FIGURE 1. Experiencing as a Circular Process

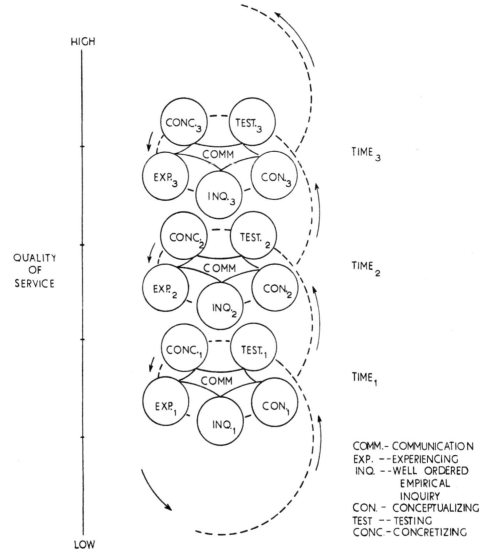

FIGURE 2. The Knowing Process

proceed successively and continuously through the phases of acting, reconnoitring or evaluating action, and planning,[7] and can be represented as in Figure 1. Floyd H. Allport[8] has suggested, in fact, that most processes in the physical and social world can be represented as self-closing circuits, and he is in the process of developing a theory of perception based upon this idea.

To complete this conception of the knowing process the final step must be to represent these several circular processes as all being interrelated with one another through the communication process and all moving in relation to one another in an ascending spiral. Figure 2 suggests such a representation. As we can see, each process as it moves through its self-repeating circuit influences all of the others; each, in turn, is affected continuously by all of the others. This representation is, of course, an idealized picture of the knowing process. It never operates as perfectly as this, for occasionally one process or another may slow down almost to a standstill, or some process may temporarily detach itself from the total structure and continue to revolve around its own axis without affecting the other processes to an appreciable extent.

In terms of this conception it becomes clear that both practice and theory building are interdependent and indispensable aspects of the knowing process. It follows, too, that practice and theory building must be regarded as two essential aspects of the role of every member of a profession, although members will inevitably participate in these activities in different ways and to different degrees depending upon their interests, aptitudes, and training.

To recapitulate, and summarize what has been said so far, it is contended that professional practice involves believing, knowing, and doing. Each is essential; all are interdependent. Knowledge, obviously, is the product of the knowing process, and the latter has been seen as a complex structure consisting of the activities of experiencing, empirical inquiry, conceptualizing, testing and concretizing—all functioning through the communication process as a dynamic whole.

---

[7] Kurt Lewin suggested this form of representation in "Frontiers in Group Dynamics, II: Channels of Group Life; Social Planning and Action Research," *Human Relations*, 1 (1947), p. 149.
[8] Floyd H. Allport, *Theories of Perception and the Concept of Structure* (New York: John Wiley & Sons, 1955).

Chapter II

THEORY BUILDING

Theory building should be regarded by members of a profession as an activity essential to both their continued professional development and the improvement of service. Granted other favourable conditions, the quality of professional service will improve as members of a profession increase their level of understanding and skill. And understanding, in turn, will increase not only as members accumulate experience, but also as they draw upon and contribute to the development of an expanding body of theory.

The primary responsibility for building theory for a particular field of service belongs to the profession which serves that field. This is not to deny the essential auxiliary contribution of the related scientific disciplines, whose contribution is fully acknowledged and demonstrated in the later sections of this discussion. But the profession has the major responsibility, and therefore the special role of the professional in the theory building process constitutes the particular emphasis and focus of this present chapter.

CLARIFICATION OF TERMS

First, in order to be clear and precise, the particular sense in which certain terms are used herein is made explicit.

1. *Theory* is regarded as an internally consistent body of verified hypotheses. It is assumed, of course, that "verification" is provisional rather than absolute. The history of science makes such a qualification imperative, for the annals of science record numerous instances wherein that which was "true" yesterday has been replaced today by some new "truth." Hypotheses established as true according to Newtonian physics, for instance, have since been replaced by others based upon quantum physics. Frequently new truth emerges as an integration of what were regarded earlier as diametrically opposite and irreconcilable "truths." The long and bitter controversy in anthropology between Malinowski's "functionalist" school and Franz Boas' "historical" school, and the more recent controversy in social work between the functional and diagnostic theories, are cases in point. What appeared as irreconcilable differences were, or promised to be, integrated eventually into new and more comprehensive theories. Theory is dynamic and forever provisional.[1]

Conant has suggested, for this reason, that theory should always be regarded as a policy and never as a creed.[2] For to use theory as a creed would be to

[1] This point is discussed more fully by Morton I. Teicher, "Anthropology and the Functional-Diagnostic Controversy," *Social Service Review*, 27 (1953), pp. 55-61.

[2] James B. Conant, *Modern Science and Modern Man* (New York: Columbia University Press, 1952), p. 91.

assume absolute knowledge, whereas to regard it as policy is to act "as if" it were true since it has been verified only to the best of our present ability. In thus regarding theory as a policy, we remain prepared for the possibility that present theory and the policy based upon it may have to be revised in the future.

Some may contend that if theory is an internally consistent body of verified hypotheses, social work, at least at present, has no theory. This contention would be true, however, only if we were speaking of theory to encompass the whole of social work, which we are not. It is possible and proper to conceive of innumerable lesser domains within the larger social work domain. Client motivation, capacity, and opportunity might be examples of such lesser domains, and other examples might include the process of establishing a helping relationship, effecting stable adoptions, and assisting in the development of ego-strength. If these domains also proved to be beyond our present theory building power, still lesser domains within these part-domains would first have to be attacked until it did become possible to develop such internally consistent bodies of verified hypotheses. Thus, a field such as social work can and does have theory. But, inevitably, such a young profession must begin with fragments of theory, which later can be integrated into theories encompassing increasingly larger domains. Melvin H. Marx[3] has made some additional useful observations about theories, namely, that they are useless unless communicated; they are both tools and objectives; and they are always relative to the bias of their author.

2. An *hypothesis* is a provisional conjecture as to the causes or relation of phenomena. A good hypothesis is one which is in agreement with observed facts, does not conflict with any law of nature which is assumed to be true, is stated in the simplest possible terms, and permits the making of deductions which may be empirically verified.

3. A *concept* is a mental image of an action or thing. It is an idea rather than a percept, the latter being an impression of an object gained through the senses, whereas a concept is a construction of the mind. To be used in theory, a concept must define the properties which the action or thing it describes is assumed to possess and such definition must be in terms that convey a similar meaning to a number of persons. We have tended in social work to refer rather loosely to concepts and in so doing may often have been referring, not to concepts, but perhaps to democratic doctrine or to some set of principles of practice.

Lydia Nolan[4] and her students are making a valuable contribution to the field of social work in their present attempts to ferret out what are truly concepts and then to define them. So far they have been able to define precisely the concepts of self-awareness, objectivity, acceptance, and empathy. It is their intention to follow a procedure advocated by Kurt Lewin and others of developing both conceptual and operational definitions in each case. In the present stage of the Nolan studies only conceptual definitions have been developed to-

[3] Melvin H. Marx, *Psychological Theory* (New York: Macmillan, 1951).

[4] F. H. Amundrud *et. al.*, "A Study of Selected Concepts and Principles Involved in the Casework Contribution to the Helping Relationship," Part II, Group Research Project under the faculty supervision of Mrs. Lydia Nolan, School of Social Welfare, University of California, Berkeley, 1957.

gether with certain principles to guide the worker in his relationship with the client. It is their intention to proceed to the operationalizing stage as soon as they are able. As an example, acceptance has been conceptually defined as follows: "Acceptance in social casework is an attitude of disciplined concern and respect on the part of the worker for the individual and for his need to behave as he does" (p. 58). An example of the principles relating to the concept of acceptance which they have defined is as follows: "Principle 1. Worker should communicate his acceptance to the client by allowing him freedom to express or to repress his feelings and thoughts" (p. 58). There are similar definitions and principles stated for the concepts of self-awareness, objectivity, and empathy.

4. A *construct*, as it is used in this formulation, is also a concept but one of a special order. It represents a higher degree of abstraction than a simple concept. It, too, is assumed to have certain properties but the difference is that they are not so readily observable. Personality, ego, openness or closedness in systems, would thus be examples of constructs rather than concepts.

5. A *model* is a symbolic representation of a perceptual phenomenon. Paul Meadows has said that "the formulation of a model consists in conceptually marking off a perceptual complex. It involves, moreover, replacing part or parts of a perceptual complex by some representation, or symbol. Every model is a pattern of symbols, rules and processes regarded as matching, in part or in totality, an existing perceptual complex. Each model stipulates, thus, some correspondence with reality, and some verifiability between model and reality."[5]

Models vary in two ways. They vary, first, in their level of abstraction. At the lower end of the abstraction continuum are the iconic or pictorial models; in the middle ranges are the descriptive models; and at the upper end are the more abstract mathematical models. James M. Beshers explains that mathematical models "are constructed by abstracting the properties of some data by measurement, and by expressing these properties in a set of symbolic statements that include the logical relationships that hold for the entire set of statements. Any mathematical statement may be regarded as a model by identifying the symbols of the mathematical statement with some data."[6]

Models may vary, secondly, in terms of the metaphor they employ. Meadows[7] has indicated that historically the two dominant metaphors have been the organism and the machine. These have exchanged dominant positions, depending upon the particular cultural *milieu*. The Greeks, for example, preferred the organismic model of "system," whereas the Renaissance thinkers embraced the machine model. At present there appear to be three types—the organism, the machine, and the field—with the organism in the dominant position.

---

[5] Paul Meadows, "Models, Systems and Science," *American Sociological Review*, 22 (1957), p. 4.

[6] James M. Beshers, "Models and Theory Construction," *American Sociological Review*, 22 (1957), p. 33.

[7] The author is greatly indebted for his present understanding of the role of models in theory building to an excellent analysis of the work of Meadows and others by Wanda R. McNeill, see "Theoretical Models and Social Work" in V. Carlson *et al.*, "Social Work and General Systems Theory" (Group Research Project, School of Social Welfare, University of California, Berkeley, 1957), pp. 20-32.

Models at each level of abstraction and patterned after each different metaphor have both their values and their limitations. With respect to the level of abstraction, there are many domains in which our current level of understanding permits representation only in pictorial or descriptive terms. Development of mathematical models, while the inevitable goal, is a distant one in these domains. With respect to choice of metaphors the best strategy seems to be to use all of them as they seem appropriate. George has advocated the use of mixed metaphors but with the caution that one must at all times be aware of when and for what purpose each metaphor is being used.[8] For example, the human individual can perhaps best be represented as an organism. Certain human processes, however, are more aptly represented as feedback mechanisms patterned after the machine metaphor. Wanda McNeill concludes that for philosophical and practical reasons, the dominant model for social work should be the organismic model, with machine models being used on a very selective basis for specific purposes. Man must still be regarded as a whole being and a purposive one, or else he loses his "essence"; of lesser importance is the obvious fact that social work, also, would lose its "essence."

6. Later in this chapter and throughout Part II there are frequent references to what is called a *constructual framework*. This is simply a number of constructs organized with respect to some model. It ties all of the constructs related to a particular phenomenon together, so to speak, and shows the relation they bear to one another.

7. There are references also to *analogues* whose distinction from, and relation to, models has already been suggested. An analogue is that which is assumed to be similar in nature and function to some other thing. It is an observable example of the metaphor upon which a particular model is based. For example, Miller, in explicating the construct "open system," uses the typical modern high-speed computing machine as an analogue.[9] In so doing he is saying that an open system is like a machine of the high-speed computing type. Construction of this sort by analogy is one of the most essential tools of science,[10] although it has to be used always with great caution.

8. Finally, *conceptualizing* (in preference to the less familiar constructualizing) refers to the activity of analysing some phenomenon into its constructual and conceptual components and representing them as a dynamic whole, organized in relation to some model.

THE THEORY BUILDING PROCESS

Again for the purpose of clarity, the theory building process is discussed, in idealized terms, as a logical, linear sequence of phases. Once the process has been comprehended in this form it is easy later in the discussion to represent

[8] F. H. George, "Logical Constructs and Psychological Theory," *Psychological Review*, 60 (1953), p. 4.

[9] James G. Miller, "Toward a General Theory for the Behavioral Sciences," *American Psychologist*, 10 (1955), p. 523.

[10] Robert Oppenheimer, "Analogy in Science," *American Psychologist*, 11 (1956), pp. 127-135.

it in a form that is somewhat closer to reality—as a circular or self-repeating and spiralling process.

The Preliminary Phase

Certain preliminary steps must be taken, of course, before the actual process of theory building begins. These steps are so self-evident that possibly it is unnecessary to mention them, and they are included simply to give a more complete account of the total process. Obviously, it is necessary first to define the theory domain on which one intends to focus. It is assumed, too, that the theorist has become familiar with the phenomenon that falls within the theory domain and that he is familiar with the existing theory pertaining to it.

Identifying Inadequacies in Present Theory

After these preliminary steps have been taken, the theory building process actually begins, and the first phase is to identify the inadequacies in existing theory. Assuming that existing theory has been tested by logical, empirical, or experimental methods, attempts should be made to answer the following questions: Is there new evidence or experience which appears to challenge existing theory? Are there areas within the domain with which present theory does not deal? Are there conflicting theories about certain areas? What are the issues around which this conflict arises and what are the positions with respect to these issues? Answers to such questions will define the inadequacies and problems in present theory.

The method of analysis which Floyd H. Allport has used in preparation for his monumental work on *Theories of Perception and the Concept of Structure* is a classic example of the process here described.[11] After grouping and analysing all of the major theories of perception (and there are a great many of them), he identified thirty questions which perceptual theory of the future must attempt to answer. His approach might well serve as an example for others to follow.

Making Explicit One's Value-Orientation

Anyone who tries to explain some phenomenon inevitably does so with reference to his philosophy or value-orientation. If we try to explain human behaviour, for instance, we begin with certain assumptions about the nature and ultimate destiny of man. Approach to theory building itself will be influenced by our beliefs about the nature of knowing and the extent to which we think one can achieve certainty.

Though as scientists we strive to be objective, the fact is that we can only approach but never achieve perfect objectivity. We can comprehend only a portion of the multitude of facts and relationships in the world about us; and because of the mechanism of selective perception, we notice and remember only a portion of all that is available to us. What the theory builder looks at and perceives, then, will be greatly influenced by the society in which he lives and by his view of man and the universe, for he will tend to notice and incorporate

---

[11] Floyd H. Allport, *Theories of Perception and the Concept of Structure* (New York: John Wiley and Sons, 1955).

only that which fits, while rejecting that which violates, his philosophy or value-orientation. Furthermore, the constructs, models, and analogues he selects as the basis of his conceptual scheme will also reflect his philosophical orientation. If he believes that man is something more than a mere animal or a machine, for instance, the constructs he selects will be capable of dealing with the additional unique elements in human nature. And the hypotheses which constitute the theory will likewise reflect the theory builder's value-orientation.

A social work researcher in conversation with the author told of her experience in studying research centres in Germany several years ago. Having reviewed research in five or six important centres, she found that in no place was there even one project which was concerned with research about change, factors or forces influencing change, or potential and capacity for change in the individual. There was no idea of "from the log cabin to the White House," and therefore their studies and research had to do with identification of types, diagnosis and classification, or research in the processes of learning how one might best fulfil one's particular role in society. The social structure and social philosophy provided no place for "upward mobility," or for a wide range of change in individual behaviour or achievement.

In all his theory building, of course, the researcher tries to be objective. In collecting data to test his hypotheses, for instance, he will naturally try to construct instruments which are independent of philosophical bias and thus capable, hopefully, of correcting for it. But the important fact to remember is that the beginning phases of all theory building are value-oriented to some extent, and that consequently the theorist should make explicit his operating philosophy at the outset so that its biases and limitations may be clearly recognized by others.

Selecting Appropriate Constructs and Models

Having assessed the present state of theory within the defined domain, having identified its inadequacies, and having made his value-orientation explicit, the theorist will next select or develop appropriate constructs and models. Ideally, he will select a central integrating construct capable of encompassing the entire focal domain. The construct "field," for example, is such an integrating construct in Lewinian theory as is the construct "system" in the present formulation. In addition, he will select the other constructs required for an adequate description of the domain. The entire set of constructs, in addition to being consistent with the value-orientation and superior in theory-developing potential to those in existing theory, must constitute an integrated whole—that is, they must be fully integrated with one another and with the central integrating construct.

At the time of selecting the necessary constructs, the theory builder should also develop the theoretical models needed to define the relationships within and between the various categories of constructs. Actually, construct and model selection will take place concurrently, and each will contribute toward the other.

The final step in this phase will be to select analogues whenever it seems likely that they may contribute to a fuller understanding of the focal phenomenon. Such use of analogy has its hazards, as has been indicated, and should be used with caution. The only appropriate way to use an analogy is to consider both the positive and negative analogy between the analogue and the phenomenon with which it is compared. One should always consider the ways in which they are different as well as the ways in which they are similar. For example, it is appropriate, if one wishes, to assume that an organism acts like a machine in certain ways and unlike one in others. It could be misleading, however, to consider only the similarities. And it would be completely inaccurate and unwarranted to assume that an organism *is* a machine.

Above all, one should regard present constructs, models, analogues, and theory as provisional, fully expecting them to be replaced by superior ones in the future. They are never ends in themselves but rather a means towards understanding. The quest for understanding is a continuous process of *re-searching*.

Developing the Constructual Framework

Constructs, models, and analogues, once selected, are the materials with which the constructual framework is built. Let us imagine, for illustration, that the phenomenon about which theory is to be built is observed to possess certain properties. It can, for instance, be perceived as a whole; it has sub-parts which are related to one another; it exists in an environment; it tends to achieve a characteristic state regardless of the conditions from which it starts; and as the sub-parts work in relation to one another, the whole tends to maintain itself in something like a steady state (and incidentally, the phenomenon so described could be an individual, or it could be a human group). In this example let us assume that, these properties having been observed and contemplated as a whole, *system* has been postulated as a central integrating construct, and additional constructs to describe the observed properties have been denoted, respectively, as: sub-system, supra-system, equifinality, functional unity, and steady state. Finally, a conceptual framework is proposed when it is stated that "systems have

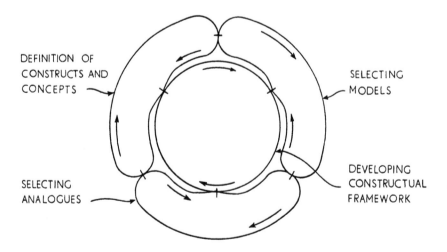

FIGURE 3. Construct, model, analogue selection, and constructual framework development as interdependent circular processes

sub-systems operating as a functional unity and as part of a supra-system which includes the system and its environment; and the whole as it functions, operates according to the principle of equifinality and tends, as well, to maintain itself in a steady state." If it can be assumed further that such a statement has been reformulated, subsequently, in terms of a theoretical model, then one would have developed the more elaborate constructual framwork of the type required for rigorous theory building.

Actually, of course, the preceding phases of construct, model, and analogue selection, and the present one of framework development take place concurrently, and in this sense might be represented most appropriately as in Figure 3. During the entire course of theory building, all four activities proceed as circular processes, and each derives from, as it also contributes to, the others.

Formulation of Hypotheses

Once a constructual framework has been developed, hypotheses may be formulated as the next step. It is important to keep two things in mind in formulating hypotheses. First, all hypotheses must be conceived within, and derived logically from, the constructual framework. And second, they must, as far as possible, be stated in terms which permit experimental verification.

The following example may illustrate how an hypothesis might be developed, keeping these two matters in mind. Let it be assumed that the hypothetical phenomenon which it was said could be comprehended by the construct *system* is, in the present instance, the staff of an agency. From what may be assumed about the nature of systems, and assuming further that the agency is a system, it would be possible to state a general hypothesis to the effect that *the structure and the functioning of the staff group as a system are interdependent.* But an hypothesis in this form cannot be put to an experimental test. It must first be translated into terms which are observable and measurable. With respect to the present example of an agency, as a sytem, one might assume that one aspect of functioning is the communication process within the staff of the agency, and a manifestation of the system's structure might be the status organization, that is, the arrangement of positions of the members in relation to one another. Assuming this, one could then restate the hypothesis as follows: *a change in the communication process will produce a change in the status organization.*

Now, while this is closer, it is still not in a form to permit experimental verification. As a further step one would have to select some observable and measurable aspect of both communication and status. Perhaps the distribution of verbal comments which members direct toward other members in an effort to influence them might be regarded as a manifestation of communication; and the organizational chart of the agency, which is the official designation of the hierarchy of staff positions, might be regarded as a manifestation of the formal status organization. One could then hypothesize that *the distribution of influence-attempts directed by the members toward one another will change whenever there is a change in structure reflected in the organizational chart.* Such an hypothesis could be tested either empirically or experimentally.

Thus, in this example, the final hypothesis has been conceived within the constructual framework, and it has been made testable, finally, as it has been expressed in observable or measurable terms. Such is the procedure that should be used in the formulation of all one's hypotheses.

It is necessary, further, in this discussion of hypothesizing to mention another related procedure which is frequently used. In the present example, for instance, one might be interested in the effect that the *size of the staff* has on its functioning. In this case, one might hypothesize that as the size of the staff increases the distribution of influence-attempts will change; also that there will be pressures exerted to change the organizational structure. In this case, size is a *variable*, in the sense that it can affect such factors as communication and status, which have been regarded not as variables but as a sub-system in the case of communication, and as a structural dimension in the case of status. Such distinctions are useful because they make for greater clarity and precision in the formulation of hypotheses.

It is perhaps worth noting that it is in this rather extended process of conceptualizing and hypothesizing that the related scientific disciplines may make important contributions. Frequently, for instance, it is possible to apply directly constructs that have already been developed. Genevieve Carter tells about one research project in which the construct *membership reference group*, already widely utilized in social psychological research, proved useful in accounting for the variability among the attitudes of pregnant mothers toward their confinement experiences in a particular hospital.[12] Another example is a recent project related to the current attempt to develop new treatment concepts in delinquency.[13] In this project Erik Erikson and Robert Merton were brought together to try to find a meeting place where the analytic concepts of personality could join with the concepts of sociology in the understanding of delinquency. Certainly, one of the times when collaboration between practitioner and social or behavioural scientist is imperative is during the process of conceptualizing and hypothesizing.

Testing Hypotheses

After the hypotheses have been formulated, the next step, obviously, is to test them. We shall forgo an extended discussion of how to conduct such tests properly. Such an elaboration is hardly necessary. Suffice it to say that they must be conducted according to the most rigorous application of the scientific method. It is at this point, too, that the greatest precautions must be taken to insure that the value biases, which may have influenced the formulation of hypotheses, are not allowed to influence the results. If such tests have been conducted in the laboratory under certain controls, one will probably also want to subject the hypotheses to additional tests in the field. Or better still, their practical implications could be explored in something approximating an ex-

[12] Genevieve W. Carter, "Theory Development in Social Work Research," *Social Service Review*, 29 (1955), p. 39.

[13] Helen L. Witmer and Ruth Kotinsky, *New Perspectives for Research on Juvenile Delinquency* (Children's Bureau Publication No. 356-1956 [Washington, D.C.: U.S. Department of Health, Education, and Welfare]).

perimental field station before they were widemy applied in regular practice. In this connection, Greenwood,[14] among others, has suggested that more schools of social work might develop and operate agencies combining the functions of training, treatment, and research. Such university-related agencies would perform one of their most useful functions in this phase of the theory building process.

Formulating Theory

Theory is formulated finally out of the results of the experimental testing of hypotheses. Great caution has to be exercised, again, at this stage of converting research findings into theoretical statements. Temptation to generalize beyond the limits of one's data is always present.

An important part of formulating theory out of research findings is the integration of the new theory with the old. Sometimes new theory will support, extend, or refine the old. Occasionally, however, new theory may challenge and bid to replace the old. Whatever the effect, it is important not merely to add theory but to *integrate* the new with that part of the old which can be retained.

Concretizing

If the scientific process were to stop at the point of theory formulation, it would have little, if any, effect on practice. In fact, the theory building process itself might even stop eventually, lacking the further stimulation of enriched experience. Thus, the act of translating theory back into practical operating terms is an integral part of the theory building process. What such translation means, simply, is to spell out for the practitioner as specifically and concretely as possible the course of action which the theory implies.

Empirical Testing and Utilization

Concretizing leads to the final phase of the theory building process, in which theory meets its crucial test and realizes its ultimate fulfilment. This is the practical test. If the new theory has been soundly conceived, eventually, if not immediately, it will begin to influence and refine practice. If, however, it is unsound, experience will reveal its weaknesses and eventually lead to its rejection or modification.

Those ideas and procedures arising from new theory which are more farreaching and radical in their effects will usually not be adopted immediately. Practitioners will want to accustom themselves to the new ideas and procedures and they will need to develop the skill required to use them. Inevitably, too, in this stage of practical utilization, experience will reveal new gaps and inadequacies in the newly developed body of theory. Such inadequacies may have arisen from faulty, incomplete, or inconsistent premises in the basic value-orientation, or they may have arisen from an unfortunate choice of constructs and models. Whatever the cause, when once again the body of existing theory is

[14] Ernest Greenwood, "Social Science and Social Work: A Theory of Their Relationship," *Social Service Review*, 29 (1955), p. 31.

examined and found inadequate, one will have come full circle, returning to the point at which the theory building process begins anew.

Theory Building as a Circular Process

What has been described as a linear sequence of phases is actually a self-closing and continuous circular process. It could be represented as the type of structure shown in Figure 1 in the opening chapter. But the fuller and more appropriate representation of the theory building process, actually, would be in the order of that shown in Figure 2. For the theory building process in reality is a *spiralling structure of interrelated circular processes.*

Chapter III

THE PATTERN OF
THEORY BUILDING IN SOCIAL WORK

From the earliest days of the profession, social work has been concerned in various ways and to varying degrees with research and theory building. The present chapter attempts to trace, briefly, the history and pattern of that concern up to the present and, further, to propose some directions which theory building in social work might profitably take in the immediate future. Recognition of two facts, namely, that social work is a profession, and that it is a profession which has followed a particular course of development, are necessary to the full comprehension and appreciation of the particular kinds of theory building activity which have been characteristic.

THEORY BUILDING IN A PROFESSION

Social work, it is rather generally agreed, is neither purely an art nor purely an applied science, but rather a *science-based art*, although Isaac Hoffman contends that today such an assertion is more a logical imperative than an empirical reality.[1] Herman Stein has said that "social work derives its knowledge from science but its spirit from philosophy, religion, ethics, moral values, and its method is derived at least in part from unexplored—or unexplorable—subtleties of human relationship. There is art in social work precisely because it is not all science, and while we must strive constantly to enhance the scientific base of our work, we would not wish to eliminate, even if we could, the aesthetic or the ethical component."[2] Stein might have added that because there is also the component of skill in professional practice it can never be a pure or even an applied science but must inevitably be essentially and ideally a science-based art.

Strictly speaking, rather than to refer to the theory *of* an art it would seem more appropriate to speak of theory *for* an art—theory which provides the understanding essential to the practice of the art. It is in this latter sense, consequently, that we conceive of social work theory in this formulation. The body of theory which provides the understanding upon which the practice of social work is based will include knowledge about the realities with which social work deals, the methods it employs in performing its function, and the means by which social workers acquire the attitudes, knowledge, and skill essential to professional practice.

[1] Isaac L. Hoffman, "Research, Social Work and Scholarship" (paper presented before Prof. R. Clyde White's Advanced Seminar in Social Work Research at the School of Applied Social Science, Western Reserve University, Cleveland, April 12, 1955).

[2] Herman D. Stein, "Social Science and Social Work Practice and Education," *Social Casework*, 36 (1955), p. 148.

FROM CRAFT TO PROFESSION

Professions usually follow one of two patterns in their course of development. On one hand, a field of science may first be developed, after which a profession is established to apply the knowledge that has been accumulated. Such was the case in professions such as the ministry and, more recently, clinical psychology. On the other hand, practice may begin as a primitive craft and develop into a profession as theoretical knowledge gradually replaces empiricism. Medicine is an example of this latter course of development.[3]

It seems clear that social work, also, belongs in this second category. It began as a craft and has developed into a profession. Grace Coyle has suggested that the marks of a profession are: (1) the development of a tested body of knowledge; (2) the establishment of standards; (3) the growth of professional consciousness; and (4) the making of a significant contribution to society.[4] Certainly social work has made tremendous gains in all these respects from its earlier primitive beginnings, and few today would dispute its claim to professional status.

That social work has developed from craft to profession has been stressed here because there are certain consequences of this fact that have influenced the present direction and quantity of theory building in the profession. One consequence, as Hoffman points out, has been the inevitable and persistent struggle between those who prefer to have social work remain a craft and those who prefer to have it become a profession. The former tend to operate on the basis of empiricism and intuition, distrusting and often resisting the intrusion of science, and the latter strive to develop a scientific basis for practice. Undoubtedly, some energy that otherwise might have been expended in theory building has been dissipated in this internal struggle.

Another consequence has been that the "profession builders" in their eagerness and impatience to attain professional status have sometimes tried to build social work theory by adopting *in toto* ready-made theories from other fields and professions. As a result, the profession has tended to over-rely upon certain bodies of theory to the neglect of others. Alfred Kahn sums up the present situation as follows:

> . . . social work knowledge is, at the present time, an amalgam of several different things: (1) propositions borrowed from, or markedly like those of, psychiatry and some branches of psychology; (2) propositions, fewer than in (1) borrowed from, or markedly like those of sociology, social anthropology and a scattering from other fields; (3) apparently original propositions about how to do certain things in case work, group work and community organization; (4) methods, techniques, and attitudes clearly derived from the fields of administration, statistics and social research; (5) propositions about how to do things apparently derived from, or markedly like those of progressive education.[5]

The hazard in this situation does not reside in the possibility that these particular fields should not have been used as sources for social work theory. They

---

[3] Hoffman, "Research, Social Work and Scholarship," p. 2.

[4] Grace L. Coyle, "On Becoming Professional," *Group Experience and Democratic Values* (New York: Woman's Press, 1947), pp. 81-97.

[5] Alfred J. Kahn, "The Nature of Social Work Knowledge," *New Directions in Social Work,* ed. Cora Kasius (New York: Harper and Bros., 1954), p. 197.

are all entirely appropriate sources. It is rather that a profession cannot build its theory this way. While it can and must utilize the insights and methodology from related fields, ultimately it must formulate its theory in terms of its own function.

Another danger is that the profession may operate on the false assumption that the knowledge it requires is already available and fully developed in other related sciences. In the social sciences, upon which social work largely relies, this is a myth; for while there are in the social sciences some well-developed areas, there are many other areas in the social sciences which at present are under-developed and to which, in fact, social work experience itself could probably contribute more than it would receive.

Another consequence of the impatience to achieve professional status through the rapid acquisition of a body of knowledge has been the tendency among some members of the profession to regard theory as a creed rather than a policy. Instead of respecting the dictum to "know all theories, love some, and wed none," there has been a tendency to know, love, and wed one or another theoretical system to the exclusion of all others and to regard the chosen one as revealed truth. Such a course, naturally, is satisfying, since it usually makes for orderliness, definiteness, and conviction, but unfortunately, because of its exclusiveness, it is likely to lead toward sterility and stagnation. In contrast, an approach which regards today's theory as a policy—as the closest approximation to the truth that has yet been achieved—is often disorderly and indefinite, but it does, in addition to its other growth-producing advantages, permit and foster change in the face of new experience.

Theory Building in Social Work—Past to Present

In tracing the history of theory building in social work it is interesting to recall that in the early days, organized social work was very closely related to the social sciences. Stein reminds us that the first national conferences of social work in the 1870's were sponsored by the then "American Social Science Association."[6] Although the National Conference of Social Work was established independently in 1879, social work continued to draw heavily on sociology, economics, and political science until about 1920. At this point social work became somewhat less interested in contact with the social sciences and more concerned with incorporating the insights of dynamic psychology into its theory and practice. The field was concerned primarily with defining the role of the social worker, or perhaps more accurately, the roles of social caseworker, social group worker, and community organization worker.

The great depression of the 1930's marked an important turning point in the theory building and research activities of the profession. Not only did it broaden enormously the public's conception of the scope of social welfare and the pattern of the social services, but, as Hoffman has pointed out,[7] it opened up new

---

[6] Stein, "Social Science and Social Work Practice and Education," p. 147.
[7] Hoffman, "Research, Social Work and Scholarship," p. 4.

areas for study and provided, through such programmes as the Work Projects Administration's research projects in the United States, new means for carrying on work that would otherwise have been impossible. Some of these projects contributed significantly to the advancement of knowledge although they were hampered in making their potential contribution, he believes, by the fact that "a raw research empiricism was being applied to an equally raw service pragmatism."

In the period prior to the Second World War, activity in the realm of research was characterized by efforts to reawaken a consciousness of research in the social worker; a struggle to formalize procedures for estimating the volume of social services; fact-finding surveys; exploratory studies undertaken with the hope that what was found would prove worth finding; and a few studies attempting to apply the best known methods of research to the unknown content of social work phenomena.[8]

Significant advances toward theory building on a more sophisticated level began at the close of the Second World War, and perhaps the Workshop on Social Work Research held at Western Reserve University in 1947 might be regarded as a landmark of this new period. Since that time there have been some notable developments which augur well for the future. Programmes at the doctoral level in a dozen schools of social work in the United States and Canada are developing persons capable of giving leadership to an advanced level of theory building. A number of scientists from allied fields have become identified with, and are devoting their talents to, the field of social work. Many of those responsible for the research component in social work education have also embarked upon long-term programmes of research oriented toward, and contributing to, a growing body of theory. And, more and more, welfare councils and national agencies are developing and staffing research departments as qualified personnel become available.

While these are encouraging developments which hold promise of a brighter future, it must be acknowledged, nevertheless, that their full impact is yet to be felt in the field at large. One feels disposed to agree with Greenwood's observation that "if we were to take what today passes for practice theory in social work ... we would find that it has been built up in the main in a trial-and-error, crudely empirical, and highly pragmatic manner."[9] By and large, he contends, practice theory has been constructed by practitioners who were untutored in the canons of scientific inquiry and who have relied solely upon the richness of their insights and the wisdom derived from day-to-day experience.

There has been some ordering of experience, although this has not yet been fully exploited as the basis for empirical inquiry of the order described in chapter I. A study by Saloshin in the group work area,[10] and a book by Ross

---

[8] *Ibid.*, p. 3.

[9] Ernest Greenwood, "Social Science and Social Work: A Theory of Their Relationship." *Social Service Review*, 29 (1955), p. 27.

[10] Henrietta E. Saloshin, "Development of an Instrument for the Analysis of the Social Group Work Method in a Therapeutic Setting" (unpublished Doctoral Dissertation, School of Social Work, University of Minnesota, 1954).

in community organization,[11] and others by Aptekar[12] and Perlman[13] in casework might be cited as examples of important recent contributions to ordering experience. Formulations such as these, used as the basis for systematic research programmes, could and should contribute important additions to the body of social work theory.

As far as theory building at the conceptualizing level is concerned, the picture is not nearly so encouraging. Certainly, such activity has become one of the most pressing needs in the field. Some ordering of experience according to concepts currently being used in the field is always possible, but eventually such activity must come to a standstill unless new integrating and higher-level constructs are formulated. The apparent paucity of newly acquired insights and of newly formulated principles, if the content of recent literature on social work practice is a true indication, would suggest that we have reached that point of diminishing return in social work. One of the more urgent needs, therefore, for both theory building and practice is the development of what Conant has called "concepts on a grand scale."

THE FUTURE

The direction and pace of theory building in the immediate future will depend, in part, upon the manner in which the profession resolves certain questions it will eventually be obliged to consider. Because of their relevance to this formulation, three such questions, among the many other important questions which might be noted, are raised for consideration here.

Social Science and Social Work

The first is the matter of deciding what should be the proper relation between the social sciences and social work. Many types of relationship have been suggested. Among them is one which might best be described as *division of responsibility*. Social scientists, it contends, should develop the theory, and either they or the practitioners should translate it into the principles of practice. Such an approach is not likely to be very effective, assuming the unlikely possibility that it would ever be attempted. Scientists rarely, if ever, consciously develop theory for specific fields of practice, and furthermore it is difficult, if not impossible, to develop theory in a vacuum. Theory for practice must be developed in relation to practice.

Another version of this same approach is the idea of making social scientists of practitioners, or at least making them "knowledgeable in the social sciences." While such a suggestion has merit and certainly should be encouraged to the fullest extent possible, it will not, in itself, guarantee the development of theory building in social work at the level that is herein advocated. Greenwood has

---

[11] Murray G. Ross, *Community Organization—Theory and Principles* (New York: Harper and Bros., 1955).

[12] H. H. Aptekar, *The Dynamics of Casework and Counseling* (Boston: Houghton Mifflin, 1955).

[13] Helen H. Perlman, *Social Casework—A Problem-Solving Process* (Chicago: University of Chicago Press, 1957).

noted two serious obstacles.[14] First, there is the communication barrier which most social workers encounter when they try to comprehend social science material; and second, the non-practical form in which most social science theory is cast.

The approach which is currently receiving the strongest support and the one which is advocated in this formulation is collaboration between social scientists and practitioners. Such an approach has already been fully outlined and has actually been demonstrated.[15] It demands that theory building be done with continual reference to the practice setting, and that social scientists and practitioners collaborate at all phases in the process. Naturally, one or the other will have the more active role in particular phases, but there is never a point at which both are not making some contribution.

Henry S. Maas has made a number of useful suggestions concerning the strategy of such collaboration. He believes first that social work practitioners must become clearer and more explicit about their identity. Toward furthering this end he suggests that "social work is *not*, like the behavioural sciences, interested in understanding man under any and all conditions. Rather social work's concern is with man's behaviour in response to stressful conditions. Social work's basic knowledge is focused, then, on the dynamics of stressful situations and especially on ways of preventing or ameliorating some of these conditions and their effects on man."[16] After enumerating a number of types of conditions which induce stress in man he indicates, by way of example, the specific bodies of knowledge in the behavioural sciences to which one might refer in trying to understand, for instance, the nature and consequences of stress arising from threats to physical integrity. We would contend that before there can be fruitful collaboration there must be more of this kind of conceptual clarification of the social worker's role and focus. The behavioural scientist can, of course, assist in this process as well and need not wait to make his contribution until such clarification has been accomplished.

The kind of research-teaching-practice agency in which, among other settings, such collaborative activity could proceed with great facility has already been discussed in the previous chapter. Such activity, however, is not wholly dependent upon the development of these specialized agencies. Every agency is potentially a practice research centre.

Theory as Policy

It is always dangerous to over-generalize, but it seems fairly safe to assume that in every practitioner there is a tendency—perhaps more in some than in others—to regard past and present theory, as was noted earlier, as a creed. This is the

[14] Greenwood, "Social Science and Social Work," p. 29.

[15] Memorandum on the "Faculty Seminar on the Research Basis of Welfare Practice: A Project Sponsored by the Russell Sage Foundation in Cooperation with the School of Social Work and Department of Sociology, University of Michigan" (Oct., 1952, mimeo.); Otto Pollak, "Relationships between Social Science and Child Guidance Practice," *American Sociological Review*, 16 (1951), pp. 61-67.

[16] Henry S. Maas, "Problems in the Use of the Behavioral Sciences in Social Work Education" (paper presented at the Annual Program Meeting of the Council on Social Work Education, Los Angeles, Jan. 1957).

"conserving" attitude of which necessarily, and happily, there is some trace in everyone, and without which there would be chaos.

Advancement, however, requires a more searching attitude which would regard theory as tentative and would hold, therefore, that present theory should be used only as a policy—as the present best basis for action and decision. It is the contention of this present formulation that the profession should do what it can to foster a larger measure of the provisional and the theory-as-policy attitude in its members as one means of promoting the acceleration of theory building activity.

The Focus of Theory Building

There is also the question of where, among all the innumerable alternatives. theory building in social work should focus in the immediate future. There have been many proposals. Greenwood, for one, regards the construction of diagnostic and treatment typologies for social work and the analysis of the value implications of social work theory as two of the most urgent tasks for the immediate future.[17] As previously indicated, Maas has suggested that one typology, at least, might be organized in relation to the concept of stress. Carter has demonstrated most effectively from the experience of the research department she directed how much can be contributed to theory by the empirical findings arising from studies made in response to the practical research questions which agencies raise.[18] Others believe that the most urgent research task is to develop techniques for evaluating service. Hoffman thinks that while proposals of this latter type are laudatory, since they indicate the willingness of practitioners to subject their work to penetrating analysis, they are probably premature.[19] Before such techniques can be developed, he believes, much more must be known about the realities of social work, that is, the individuals, the groups, the communities, and the problems with which social work helps them to deal.

In view of the present rather primitive state of social work theory, probably any aspect which a person, because of his interest, would choose to explore would be a worthwhile place for him to become involved in the theory building process. It seems inevitable that choice based on interest will be the course that most will follow in any case. But this fact makes it all the more imperative that the profession develop adequate means for co-ordinating and integrating the theoretical contributions that will accrue from such a diversity of interests. The present professional journals will, undoubtedly, soon prove to be inadequate for this purpose, and additional ones will have to be developed. Certainly, this has been the experience of every other profession. Perhaps, also, special workshops and more time at regional and national conferences will have to be devoted to symposia which can integrate and summarize theory in particular areas as it accumulates.

Now, to recapitulate briefly what has been said in Part I. Professional practice

---

[17] Greenwood, "Social Science and Social Work," p. 30.

[18] Genevieve W. Carter, "Theory Development in Social Work Research," *Social Service Review*, 29 (1955), p. 41.

[19] Hoffman, "Research, Social Work and Scholarship."

is seen as a combination of believing, knowing, and doing. Knowledge is acquired through both scientific and non-scientific knowing, represented here as a spiralling structure of interrelated circular processes. An approach to theory building in which practitioner and scientist may collaborate at every stage has been advocated as the one which will best serve to improve social work service and thus enhance the social work profession.

Part II

THEORY BUILDING IN SOCIAL WORK

INTRODUCTION

Had the theory building process, as described in Part I, been fully apparent from the beginning of this study, the form and substance of Part II might have been somewhat different. Actually, the total process, as here conceived, became clear only after the effort had been made to accomplish certain of its parts. For this reason, and also because of the limitations of time and resources, Part II is the report of an attempt to accomplish only a portion of a complete theory building cycle. A domain is defined and its theory needs identified; an attempt is made to formulate the value-orientation with respect to that domain; one among a number of possible integrating constructs and several derivative constructs are chosen; and, finally, an analogue is proposed as a method of representing and illuminating the various constructs.

This is as far as the process is carried in the present project. There has been no attempt, to the time of writing, to select or develop a theoretical model and, consequently, it has not yet been possible to build a fully elaborated constructual framework. Nor has it been possible to formulate and test any series of hypotheses, since the latter properly may be conceived only within a framework. Thus, with respect even to this limited domain, only a few steps have been taken along the long road that, hopefully, may eventually contribute to the larger body of social work theory.

THE CHOSEN DOMAIN

As previously noted in the introduction to Part I, the ultimate choice of domain of the present project stemmed from the conviction that there is, in reality, a social worker role—that there is a particular function the methods of which are fundamentally similar whether the social worker is working with individuals, groups, or larger communities.

Maas and Wolins have defined social work as the "prevention and alleviation of the socially and psychologically damaging effects of crisis situations,"[1] and presumably they would regard the function of the social worker as that of facilitating these processes of prevention and alleviation. This is consistent with a formulation by Greenwood[2] following Bisno,[3] to the effect that the function of the social worker may be defined as that of helping people to achieve relation-

---

[1] Henry S. Maas and Martin Wolins, "Concepts and Methods in Social Work Research," *New Directions in Social Work*, ed. Cora Kasius (New York: Harper and Bros., 1954), p. 215.

[2] Ernest Greenwood, "Social Science and Social Work—A Theory of Their Relationship," *Social Service Review*, 29 (1955), p. 24.

[3] Herbert Bisno, *The Philosophy of Social Work* (Washington, D.C.: Public Affairs Press, 1952), chap. i.

ships conducive to the realization of their potential as human beings, in a manner consistent with cultural patterns and values; and further, that social workers function principally when such relationships have actually broken down, or are likely to break down, doing so (a) by helping to create desirable resources in society or by marshalling existing social resources and (b) by helping people to utilize such resources. It follows, then, that the *role* of social worker is the totality of behaviours which the profession, acting on behalf of society, prescribes for persons occupying the position and performing the preventive and problem-alleviating functions of social work.

Relationship is the essence of social work, being both its object and its means. For the objective of social work, as already noted, is to help clients establish and maintain appropriate relationships with those about them and, furthermore, the relationship which the social worker establishes with the client, and the worker's influence upon the client's other relationships, are the means by which the social worker performs his function.

While most social workers would insist that the ultimate client is always an individual, the object of his work may be, in fact, an individual, a group, or some larger complex. Frequently, moreover, the social worker's immediate object may be another individual, group, or community with which he is working on behalf of a client. Whatever the case, aiding the establishment and utilization of effective relationships is his principal objective.

This formulation contends that before there can be a significant extension of theory about the social worker's role, it is necessary to develop a *common method of conceiving the client*—equally applicable whether the client, in a given instance, happens to be an individual, a group, or a community. Only when such a common conception has been developed can the essence of the worker's actions in the total social work process be identified with any greater degree of incisiveness, and studied with any greater insight and understanding than is possible at present.

Present theory in this domain is far from adequate; its various facets are rather unevenly developed and imperfectly integrated. On one hand, representations of the individual in terms of his bio-social origins, and representations of his physical and emotional development in terms of the psycho-sexual phases of the life cycle, render a fairly adequate conception of the individual as a dynamic organism. On the other, however, comparable representations of the group, or of larger complexes such as interrelated groups and communities, are far less adequate. Social work theory, for the most part, has considered the group and the community *as they affect the individual,* but has tended to ignore them as dynamic functioning realities in themselves. This, of course, is not surprising, since the social sciences have only recently undertaken the task of conceptualizing the *dynamics* in contrast to the *structure* of groups and communities.

Perhaps the greatest inadequacy in this theory domain is the lack of a satisfactory way of conceptualizing the social work process and the larger complex in which it occurs, a way, that is, of representing social work with individuals —in groups—in communities. With the conceptual schemes that are currently available we are incapable of doing much more than regard our work with individuals, groups, and communities as rather different and discontinuous processes. It is interesting to note, in this connection, that the social work profession actually has no image of a social worker. It has fairly clear images of the social caseworker, and the social group worker, and a rather vague one of the community organization worker; it has developed social casework, social group work, and community organization as three separate methods in social work. What is lacking and what is critically needed is an image of a *social worker* and a conception which would permit a departure from the traditional casework, group work, and community organization methods to that of the *social work method.*

Extending this idea one step further, there would seem to be a need, also, for a way to conceive of the medium in which the social work method operates. It might be conceived, for instance, as a network of relationships or as a continuous complex consisting of individuals—in groups—in communities. Such a conception would have to be sufficient to permit development of theory about the nature of the total complex, as well as its sub-parts, and of the social worker's function in relation to both the whole and any of the parts. It would have to explain, too, what the worker does within the complex and the effects of his participation. This is the theory domain and the task to which the present project is directed.

Chapter IV

PHILOSOPHICAL BASE

Theory building, in its early stages, is inevitably a subjective and value-oriented process. Because this is so, and since the theorist wants his theory to be as objective and value-free as possible when it is eventually developed, he tries to do what he can to take full cognizance of his biases. One means to this end is to make his philosophy explicit at the outset.

A theorist's philosophy has both its personal and its social aspects. His choice from among alternative positions on relevant philosophical questions, and the rationale for his choice, are his own. In this sense his philosophy is personal. But, at the same time, it has undoubtedly been influenced and fashioned by his relations with others with the result that his philosophy is probably also similar, in many respects, to that of many others. This is its social aspect.

In the present chapter, an attempt has been made to describe briefly those areas of philosophy underlying the present formulation which are relevant to the chosen theory domain. Almost inevitably, any such statement is a reflection of the philosophical climate in which it was conceived. Thus, it is not surprising that in this statement, conceived within the sphere of influence of Western philosophy in general and North American in particular, there is a strong emphasis upon the importance of the individual. The statement, moreover, is probably fairly representative of the philosophical position of a substantial number of social workers, since it has been formulated, for the most part, through interaction within the profession.

A number of fundamental philosophical questions are raised in the course of this chapter. As is always the case with such questions, a person may take any one of a number of positions with respect to them. What is stated here is the present position on which this formulation is based. It is realized and fully acknowledged, of course, that certain other members of the profession might wish to take a somewhat different position in certain cases. In fact, it is precisely for this reason that such strong emphasis is laid upon the importance, for all those involved in theory building, of making their philosophical positions explicit at the outset, as is done in the present instance.

On Theory Building and the Possibility of Knowing

In any project directed toward the pursuit of knowledge, the first question that must surely arise concerns the extent to which it is actually possible to attain knowledge. Are there universals which exist outside the mind, as the realists believe, or are there, as the nominalists hold, no such universal essences in reality? Can we know anything with certainty, or may we only approach and never attain certain knowledge?

While such questions will need to remain forever open, the work of the world requires that one take at least a tentative position in relation to them. In this instance, for example, we are inclined to the view that there *are* universals which exist outside the mind but that we do not, nor will we ever, fully comprehend them. All that we can ever achieve is a closer and closer approximation to the universal essences of reality. Knowledge, therefore, can only be stated in terms of probabilities, and never in absolute terms. Indeed, it is for this reason that the wisdom of using theoretical knowledge more as a policy than as a creed was stressed earlier. In the pursuit of knowledge the old frequently has to give way to the new.

To raise another question which is particularly relevant to the present project—is it true, as the pluralists believe, that there will always have to be separate theories to explain the physical and the non-physical worlds, or is it possible, as the unificationists prefer to believe, that there is in the universe only one basic form of order which is equally applicable both to the physical and to the non-physical?

Our inclination is toward the unificationist view, in this instance, although we agree fully with Rice's conclusion that:

> We are simply not in a position to decide at all assuredly the issue between pluralism with respect to principles and the possibility of unification. Both are open possibilities. The latter offers the best hope of satisfying our deep-seated demand for order within the moral domain, yet it cannot be said to have been established as more than a possibility. There is still the alternative to be taken seriously in morals as in physical science, that affairs are not wholly tidy and cannot be made so by thought, that there is an ultimate residue of chaos or loose play in their structure.[1]

It follows, of course, that those who take the unificationist position will also support the view that the various physical and non-physical scientific disciplines constitute an interdependent whole and that as such they are capable of contributing to one another's fund of knowledge. There would seem to be some support for such a contention in the fact that frequently several sciences have "discovered," independently, the same phenomenon or principle. Surely this is more than a mere coincidence, and suggests, at least, that a theory developed in one field might serve to suggest working hypotheses whose utility and generality could be determined by applying and testing them in other fields.

ON THE NATURE OF LIFE IN THE UNIVERSE [2]

Since the present project is concerned ultimately, if not immediately, with man as a living organism functioning in a particular kind of universe, it may be useful to indicate the view of living things and of the universe which underlies this formulation.

It is a widely accepted scientific fact that throughout the universe in both its

[1] Philip Blair Rice, *On the Knowledge of Right and Wrong* (New York: Random House, 1955), p. 268.

[2] The author's philosophical position with respect to this question and others has been greatly influenced by the thinking of numerous individuals but in particular by the 1957 Berkeley research group.

living and its non-living aspects there is a process in operation tending towards de-organization, the elimination of differences, and towards a completely homogeneous state. Carnot, Joule, and Kelvin defined this fact in the Second Law of Thermodynamics. Variously stated, it holds that a certain quantity called entropy, or degree of de-organization, never decreases but tends to increase to a maximum until the process in which it is operating reaches a state of equilibrium. A ghost town rotting into the ground, the human body returning to dust after death, a tea kettle cooling on the stove until it reaches room temperature—these are all examples of this fact of nature.

Entropy is at work in all of nature, in both living and non-living matter. In the former, however, another force is at work, a force towards organization, or negative entropy. In any living organism positive entropy and negative entropy are in a state of contention. If negative entropy greatly outweighs the positive entropy, growth is rapid; when they are more in balance, growth is slow; when life ceases, negative entropy has ceased and positive entropy has assumed full reign. Thus, if life in the whole or any part of the universe is to continue, negative entropy must at least be maintained.

The Nature of the Universe

Of the many diverse theories of the universe developed through the ages, the most compatible, for us, is a modern view[3] supporting the idea of the continuous creation of a continually expanding universe and contending that the universe has been and always will be an open system.

On the Nature of Human Nature

It is the contention of the present formulation that such speculations concerning the nature of the universe and life within it are not irrelevant but essential to a comprehension of man, the principal concern of social work. In fact, there are certain questions concerning the nature of human nature which are inextricably related to such cosmological considerations. What is the essence of humanness? What is man's position, his function, and his destiny in the universe?

The position which is taken here follows from certain assumptions about the unique endowments of man—in particular those which differentiate him from the animals. Humans are more than animals—more in the sense that, unlike animal, they must by nature transcend the role of the creature, the accidental character and passivity of their existence, and become *creators*. Man is not content merely to adjust to his environment. He is relentlessly driven by his own nature to create a more perfect relation between himself and his environment. Man is forever in the process of approaching the state which distinguishes his species.[4] But perhaps the principal characteristic differentiating man from all other living species is his ability to derive abstract concepts from experience, to represent these abstractions symbolically, to manipulate his symbols and through their use to develop and exchange ideas with other men. By the use

---

[3] Fred Hoyle, *The Nature of the Universe* (New York: Harper and Bros., 1950), chap. IV.

[4] This is the view so eloquently developed by Erich Fromm in his book, *The Sane Society* (New York:Rinehart and Co., 1955), p. 36.

of this conceptualizing ability, man is able to acquire and transmit knowledge and to gain increasing control over his environment.

Of considerable importance in social work is the question of man's position and function in the universe. Is man, or is he not, the centre of the universe and thus the end for which it exists? In support of the anthropocentric view, it seems logical that one so richly endowed must have special obligations and might perhaps occupy a special position in the universe. In this formulation, however, the anthropocentric view is rejected. Despite the fact that man undoubtedly has special obligations because of his unique endowments, he need not for this reason be regarded as the centre of the universe. Man, as a species, is regarded as one among many forms of life all of which function in relation to one another as a dynamic whole. Since all the species are essential, none can be regarded as occupying the centrally important position. To use an analogy, in the human individual do we regard the heart as central; or the brain; or the glands? No, because all functioning together with numerous other physiological sub-systems are essential to life. So it is with man in the universe.

What, then, will we say of the dignity of man? The majority, at least of North American social workers, would insist that by virtue of his unique endowments man has a particular dignity. And we would agree with such a view although choosing to express it in a somewhat different way. Certainly, man has great worth, at least potentially, and consequently should be treated at all times with dignity. The respect which men command in their own right must be earned, however, as they fulfil their obligations. Man has no inalienable rights except possibly the right to pursue his own destiny. What many would refer to as rights, may, perhaps, be regarded more appropriately as conditions— conditions which increase the possibility of man fulfilling his obligations as a human being. Such conditions in the physical realm, of course, would include adequate food, clothing, shelter and protection from violence and disease; and in the psychological realm would include order, freedom of opinion, some security combined with an element of risk, and some of both private and collective property, to name but a few.[5]

Although we may refer to man as a species, the fact of his infinite variability within the species should not be inadvertently overlooked. Kluckhohn and Murray[6] have said that "every man is in certain respects (a) like all other men, (b) like some other men, and (c) like no other man." Thus, while social work helps people to deal with the stressful conditions that beset them, it always tries, at the same time, to regard each person or group of persons individually, and to work with them accordingly.

ON THE SOCIAL WORK PROCESS

Social work has been defined as the prevention and alleviation of the socially

---

[5] For an excellent discussion of this matter of rights and obligations the reader is referred to Simone Weil, *The Need for Roots* (London: Routledge and Kegan Paul), 1952.

[6] Clyde Kluckhohn and Henry A. Murray, *Personality in Nature, Society and Culture* (2nd ed.; New York: Alfred A. Knopf, 1953), p. 53.

and psychologically damaging effects of crisis situations. What, then, are the values which ought to guide the social worker as he participates in the promotion of these processes? Certainly the most succinct and perhaps the most apt formulation is the oft-quoted statement that social workers "help people to help themselves." Basic to this view, of course, is the principle of self-determination which holds that, as far as possible, every individual ought to be able to claim, "I am the master of my fate: I am the captain of my Soul." Social workers try to avoid making decisions for people and try instead to help them develop their own insight, sufficient to enable them to make decisions which will be in their own best interest as well as that of the larger social complex of which they are a part.

Bertha Reynolds[7] has said that you cannot produce growth in any living thing; you can only co-operate with it. Thus, to promote growth, the social worker relies more upon environmental manipulation and the development of insight and capacity in people than upon methods of imposition.

If we grant the assumption that all humans are continually approaching but never quite achieving their proper state, it follows that everyone will experience some degree of disturbance or disquietude. A certain degree of such disturbance is probably desirable and essential to growth since it motivates the individual to explore, to strive, and to create. Yet, at times, such disturbance may reach a critical point beyond which it overpowers and immobilizes the individual. Growth may be arrested, too, because necessary resources are not available, or the individual is unable to make full use of what is available to him. One or more of his physiological or psychological processes may be temporarily or permanently impaired. These are some of the stress-producing conditions to which Maas refers. Whatever the situation, it is the social worker's function to assist the individual in achieving the closest approximation of which he is capable to the proper condition of human beings.

Finally, it is assumed that human behaviour is always the result of the interaction between the biological organism and its environment. Indeed, certain facts of his behaviour can be understood only in terms of the nature of the interaction between these two components. The social worker acts further upon the assumption that every individual is in an interdependent relationship with other individuals, including the worker; that he is a part of a number of interlocking networks of interaction (groups); and that certain dimensions of his behaviour can be understood only in terms of the structure and function of these networks, and of the individual's position and role in them.

The worker is a part of the network of interaction and, indeed, it is through it that he performs his function. By a conscious and controlled use of self he affects the quality of relationship between himself and the members; and in a similar way he also affects the relationships among the several members of the interaction network.

Each of the values which have been stated or implied in this brief account of the philosophy underlying this formulation has influenced the approach to

---

[7] Bertha C. Reynolds, *Learning and Teaching in the Practice of Social Work* (New York: Farrar and Rinehart, 1942), p. 230.

theory building that is advocated here. They have influenced, as well, the choice of the particular construct which, hopefully, may be used in conceptualizing the social medium in which social work occurs. However, the discussion of the way in which the latter has been derived from this underlying value orientation must await the introduction and elaboration of the systems construct.

Chapter V

SYSTEM: THE CENTRAL CONSTRUCT

A constructural framework for theory building is only as good as the central construct around which it is organized. Thus, to select the proper integrating construct is probably the most important step in the entire conceptualizing phase of the theory building process. Selecting the central construct follows as the next logical step after the theory domain has been defined, its theory needs identified, and the theorist's value-orientation made explicit. Since this value-orientation defines the way he views the domain, the construct which the theorist selects for purposes of conceptualizing the domain must necessarily be expressive of, and compatible with, his value-orientation.

System, or more particularly the open, organismic type of system, is introduced and elaborated as the central integrating construct for the present theory domain. Later, its formal evaluation and justification will be made after the construct has been properly introduced and fully explicated in the present chapter.

GENERAL SYSTEMS THEORY

Within recent years an interesting new connection has developed among a particular group of scientists. Representing fields as diverse as biology, physics, political science, and psychology, to mention but a few, these scientists have become identified, now, as general systems theorists. Apparently the principal factor which has drawn them together is a series of convictions which they share in common about theory and theory building. General systems theorists believe that it is possible to represent all forms of animate and inanimate matter as systems; that all forms from atomic particles through atoms, molecules, crystals, viruses, cells, organs, individuals, groups, societies, planets, solar systems, even the galaxies, may be regarded as systems. They are impressed by the number of times the same principles have been independently "discovered" by scientists working in different fields. They are also disturbed by the waste which thus occurs when scientists have remained isolated within their own scientific spheres. They believe that the unification of theory in the physical and non-physical world is desirable and ultimately attainable, at least to some degree. Accordingly, they contend that there are properties which are common to systems of every order, although manifest in different forms, and that there are universal laws which describe the structure of systems and their manner of functioning.

General systems theory, at present, is essentially a mode of thought rather than a well-developed body of theory. There have been recent efforts, however, by the general systems theorists to organize on a more formal basis and to pursue a systematic programme of research. The Society for the Advancement of General

Systems Theory was organized in Berkeley, California, in December, 1955, and published its first yearbook in 1956.[1] Programmes of research are underway at the Center for Advanced Study in the Behavioral Sciences at Stanford and at the University of Michigan's Mental Health Research Institute. The first issue of *Behavorial Science,* a journal devoted to general systems theory, was published in January, 1956. In each locality, scientists from diverse fields are working together for a twofold purpose. By examining what has been learned in other fields they hope to discover paths to new knowledge in their own spheres; and they hope through their collaborative efforts to contribute to a growing body of unified theory.

The Nature and Variety of Systems

The "system" construct has appeared, in one form or another, in almost every area of science and from the earliest of times. Meadows has suggested that system is the master model, the primordial model from which all others have sprung.[2] Similarly, Henderson, a biologist, concludes that "it is in systems that all forms of activity manifest themselves. Therefore, any form of activity may be produced by a suitable system."[3] Of the many general definitions of system, Floyd H. Allport's is one of the more comprehensive. He says that the term may be associated with

any recognizably delimited aggregate of dynamic elements that are in some way interconnected and interdependent and that continue to operate together according to certain laws and in such a way as to produce some characteristic total effect. A system, in other words, is something that is concerned with some kind of activity and preserves a kind of integration and unity; and a particular system can be recognized as distinct from other systems to which, however, it may be dynamically related. Systems may be complex; they may be made up of interdependent sub-systems, each of which, though less autonomous than the entire aggregate, is nevertheless fairly distinguishable in operation.[4]

Somewhat more succinct is the following definition by Hall and Fagen: "A system is a set of objects together with relationships between the objects and between their attributes."[5] Perhaps the principal value of this latter definition is that it specifies the basic properties of systems. Each system consists of *objects* which are simply the parts or components of the system; there are *attributes* which are the properties of the objects; and there are *relationships* among the objects and their attributes which tie the system together.

Perhaps it is because the construct "system" is so basic and so universally applicable that it has been used so often in a loose and colloquial manner, to refer to a tremendous variety of phenomena. Even when used more precisely

---

[1] *General Systems—Yearbook of the Society for the Advancement of General Systems Theory,* eds. Ludwig von Bertalanffy and Anatol Rapoport (Ann Arbor, Mich.: Braun-Brumfield, 1956).

[2] Paul Meadows, "Models, Systems and Science," *American Sociological Review,* 22· (1957), p. 7.

[3] L. J. Henderson, *The Order of Nature* (Cambridge, Mass.: Harvard University Press, 1917), p. 172.

[4] Floyd H. Allport, *Theories of Perception and the Concept of Structure* (New York: John Wiley and Sons, 1955), p. 469.

[5] A. D. Hall and R. E. Fagen, in *General Systems—Yearbook of the Society for the Advancement of General Systems Theory,* eds. Ludwig von Bertalanffy and Anatol Rapoport, p. 18.

in theory construction there has been great variation in usage. James G. Miller, in a review of Grinker's *Toward a Unified Theory of Human Behavior,* notes that most of the theorists drawn together for the conferences of which the book is a report converged upon the systems construct for purposes of exploration, but, at the same time, used it in different ways.[6] Miller was able to identify in the conference presentations and discussions three different notions of the systems construct. There were references to *conceptual* systems—formalized in the sense ordinarily employed in mathematics; there were *"real"* systems, living or non-living—objects in physical space-time which could be observed and measured ordinarily by methods and procedures common to the natural sciences; and there were *abstracted* systems—either relationships of various sorts or classes of behaviours or relationships which could be identified in, or existed between, "real" systems.

Systems, as they have been variously used in theory building, may be distinguished in two important ways. In the first place, systems may be differentiated in terms of the models they employ for purposes of symbolization. We have already indicated in this connection that models themselves may be distinguished in two ways: (1) by their level of abstraction (pictorial, descriptive, or abstract-mathematical); and (2) by the metaphor they employ (machine, organism, field, etc.) (cf. p. 10).

Systems may vary, secondly, in terms of their inherent closedness or openness. In general, systems may be regarded as being of two types: closed or open, the major difference being that closed systems are isolated from, whereas open systems are related to and exchange matter with, their environment. A good example of a closed system is a chemical experiment in which materials are confined to a reaction vessel, and once the experiment has started there is no material exchange between the reaction mixture and its surroundings. Living organisms, on the other hand, are examples of open systems.

It should be noted here that this distinction between open and closed systems is never absolute.[7] Actually, there is no system that is completely isolated from its environment, and similarly there are living organisms which tend to act like closed systems. For example, the schizophrenic individual who at certain times and in certain areas seems to be out of touch with life around him, or a semi-isolated community of Hutterites of the type described by Eaton and Weill[8] might be taken as instances of the latter. Despite this fact, however, for the sake of greater clarity, closed and open systems are described, initially, in this chapter as if they did, in fact, exist in a pure and absolute form. Later in the formulation, the closed-open distinction will be rediscussed in terms which take account of the fact that systems are actually only open and closed to some degree.

Closed and open systems, in their hypothetical ideal state, may be differentiated also in terms of certain fundamental dynamic processes which govern

---

[6] James G. Miller, review of R. R. Grinker, "Toward a Unified Theory of Human Behavior," in *Behavioral Science,* 1 (1956), p. 321.

[7] Tsune Shirai, "Systemic Models for Social Groups," *Canadian Journal of Psychology,* 7 (1953), pp. 126-132.

[8] J. W. Eaton and R. J. Weill, *Culture and Mental Disorders* (Glencoe, Ill.: Free Press, 1955)

the operation of each. The operation of closed systems is described by the previously mentioned second law of thermodynamics, which holds that a certain quantity called entropy, or degree of de-organization in the system, tends to increase to a maximum, until eventually the process ends at a state of equilibrium. Closed systems, therefore, tend to move toward a state of maximum de-organization—toward homogeneity or the levelling of differences. Probably the ultimate example of entropy is that of the so-called heat death of the universe when all energy will presumably become degraded into evenly distributed heat of low temperature, and the whole process end.[9] A more familiar example of entropy might be the case of a tea kettle of boiling water in a closed room. When the kettle is removed from the stove it gives off heat into the atmosphere, while the atmosphere, in turn, tends to cool the water. This process continues until the water and the atmosphere reach the same temperature, at which point the process stops. Entropy, then, is the tendency toward homogeneity or a state of equilibrium.

Entropy and its tendency to increase to a maximum is also present in open systems, for the second law of thermodynamics applies to all systems, open and closed. But in the case of open systems, another force is operating, namely, that toward the attainment of higher order and heterogeneity. Thus, in open systems there are forces in play both to create and to destroy order. Bertalanffy explains the process as one where, in open systems, there is not only production of entropy or disorder but also the production of the opposite which may be called negative entropy, ordering, or organization. This is possible because living organisms import from the environment complex molecules high in free energy which are available for use in a process of progressive segregation. Open systems can balance the increase of entropy and can develop toward states of increased organization by over-compensating for entropy production through synthetic and anabolic processes.

Both closed and open systems are capable of attaining stationary states, the nature of which, however, is different, in each case. A closed system *must* eventually reach a state of equilibrium, according to the second law of thermodynamics. An open system *may*, provided certain conditions are given, attain a stationary state in which the system appears also to be constant, although maintaining its constancy in a continuous change, inflow and outflow of materials. This is called a *steady state*.[10]

The Properties of Systems in General

Before proceeding to a discussion of the kind of system which would seem to be most appropriate for purposes of theory building in social work let us consider the properties of systems in general.

Every order of system with the exception of the smallest has *sub-systems*, and all but the largest are a part of a *supra-system* consisting of the system in its

[9] Ludwig von Bertalanffy, "General Systems Theory," *Main Currents in Modern Thought,* 11 (1955), p. 77.

[10] Ludwig von Bertalanffy, "An Outline of General Systems Theory," *British Journal for the Philosophy of Science,* 1 (1950), pp. 156-157.

environment. There are factors in both the system and the environment which affect their respective structure and function. In conformity with conventional scientific usage, such factors in a system or its sub-systems are called *variables*, whereas those in the environment are called *parameters*.

Every system has a *boundary* which distinguishes it from its environment. The boundary of a system may be determined in several ways, but in every case it is an arbitrary designation. Miller has defined the boundary of a system as that region where greater energy is required for transmission across it than for transmission immediately outside that region or immediately inside it.[11] The author has suggested in an earlier formulation that the boundary of a group can be defined in terms of the amount and intensity of interaction among the members.[12] Both methods are essentially the same in that the critical value which is used to demarcate the system from its environment is an arbitrary designation. Thus, the boundary of a system has reality and utility merely as a concept in the mind of the beholder.

The *environment* of a system is everything that is external to its boundary. Higher orders of systems, consequently, are always parts of the environment of the lower orders. For each system, moreover, there may be both a proximal and a distal environment.[13] The *proximal* environment may be defined as that part of the environment of which the system is aware, whereas the *distal* environment affects the behaviour of the system but is beyond the awareness of the system.

A Choice of Model for Human Systems

After this brief preliminary excursion into the realm of general systems theory it may be useful to be reminded again that the theory domain with which the present project is concerned is the conceptual representation of the objects of the social work process, namely, human individuals—in groups—in communities who are experiencing immobilizing forms and degrees of stress. Thus, it would seem to be important at this point to specify the type of model which will likely be best suited to this particular theory domain.

Level of Abstraction

Considering the present state of our knowledge of human individuals or human collectivities such as groups and communities, the middle-range descriptive kind of models are probably the most appropriate for theory building in social work. But since the attainment of more abstract and exact models is the objective of all theory building, we, too, will want to aspire towards, and expect eventually to develop, conceptual-mathematical models for our domain. As our theory building advances this latter goal will be achieved as surely as it has been in

[11] James G. Miller, "Toward a General Theory for the Behavioral Sciences," *American Psychologist*, 10 (1955), pp. 516-517.

[12] Gordon Hearn, "Toward the Conceptualization of Social Work Practice" (Second formulation; School of Social Work, University of Toronto, mimeo.), pp. 33-34.

[13] The author is indebted to Mr. John Paul, University of Toronto, for this useful distinction.

other domains. But as it is thus achieved it will probably encompass first limited segments, and then progressively larger segments of our domain.

Choice of Metaphor

Certain characteristics of human beings must be kept in mind as one chooses a metaphor for the model of human systems. Among the more important are the following facts about human beings, as individuals or collectively: (1) Humans exchange material with their environment, material in the form of both energy and information. (2) This energy may arise either from within the system or from the environment of the system. (3) Human behaviour is purposive. (4) When considered both as individuals and as a species, humans have a characteristic state toward which they move. (5) Humans may achieve their same characteristic state from different initial conditions and from varying inputs of energy and information. (6) In the human individual as well as in human aggregations such as groups and communities there is a dynamic interplay among their essential functional processes enabling them to maintain a steady state. (7) There is a tendency in human systems toward progressive mechanization, that is, in the course of human development, certain human processes tend to operate more and more as fixed arrangements. (8) Human systems show a resistance to any disruption of their steady state. (9) They are capable, within limits, of adjusting to internal and external changes. (10) They can regenerate damaged parts. (11) They can reproduce their own kind.

It will be the contention of this formulation that human individuals and human aggregations as characterized above can most appropriately be represented, in general, as *open* systems but more particularly as *organismic* systems, the latter being regarded here as one type of open system. Werner Lutz[14] would possibly contend that to do so is an over-simplification. In his recent application of the systems construct to casework practice theory he makes the point that

> . . . empirical experience is richer than any theoretical system which attempts to describe it. A human being, at any given moment, can be alternatively described as a chemical, physical, biological or personality system, and as a participant in various social systems. No single systematic description is the "right" one to the exclusion of the others. Each is a satisfactory and desirable way, for certain scientific and practical purposes, of describing phenomena. To take the position that any single frame of reference describes a phenomenon fully and adequately is to impose on empirical experience a closure that is rightly a property only of abstract theoretical systems. Such empirical closure ultimately brings to a stop both the advance of scientific knowledge and the effectiveness of practice.

The position taken in the present formulation is that while this point which Lutz makes would seem to have complete validity, nevertheless, in the present project which is trying to develop a common way of representing human beings as individuals, or as collectivities of individuals, such as groups and communities, the organismic model seems to offer the best over-all integrating basis for such a conception. Quite likely, other models may be more usefully employed to

---

[14] Werner Lutz, *Concepts and Principles Underlying Social Casework Practice* (Washington, D.C.: National Association of Social Workers, Medical Social Work Section, 1956), p. 8. Had this provocative monograph been available earlier it would have had a measurably greater influence on this formulation. Hopefully, its influence will be manifest in the subsequent phases of the larger project.

represent the various aspects of the functioning of human individuals and aggregations; and they may very well be used within the organismic model.

THE PROPERTIES OF ORGANISMIC OPEN SYSTEMS

All that has been said of systems in general applies, of course, to open systems.
They have sub-systems; they are a part of a supra-system consisting of the
system in its environment; each has a boundary. The objects which constitute
the system and its environment have their attributes. Those pertaining to the
objects of the system are variables; those pertaining to the environment are, to
avoid confusion, parameters. Such are the characteristics common to both open
and closed systems. Open systems have certain additional properties, however,
which distinguish them from closed systems. Already mentioned are the facts
(1) that open systems exchange energy and information with their environment,
that is, they have important *inputs* and *outputs* of both energy and information,
whereas closed systems do not; (2) open systems tend to maintain themselves
in *steady states*, whereas closed systems move towards a state of equilibrium.

Bertalanffy has pointed out that the characteristics of steady states are exactly
those of organic metabolism.[15] Given a continuous flow of materials, a constant
ratio among the components of the system is maintained. *The composition of
the system is independent of, and maintained constant in, a varying import of
materials.* A burning candle, while not an organism,[16] is perhaps one of the best
illustrations of an open system maintaining itself in a steady state. Allport,
following Köhler's[17] earlier use of this example explains the process as one in
which the flame of the candle when first lighted is small but grows quickly to its
normal size and maintains that size as long as the candle lasts, that is, as long
as the "food" for the flame remains available.[18]

After any disturbance, a system tends to re-establish a steady state. When
any component is added, the organism can react in such a way as to re-establish
a steady state similar to the original. If the stimulus is prolonged, however, or
if external conditions change in any major way, the system can react in such
a way as to establish another steady state.[19] Thus, another of the properties of
open systems is the process of *self-regulation*, a characteristic with important
implications for social work theory and for social work education.

Closely related to the concept of steady state is another called *equifinality*,
which simply means achieving identical results from different initial conditions.
Bertalanffy has noted that equifinality in open systems is another of the properties which distinguish them from closed systems:

---

[15] Ludwig von Bertalanffy, "The Theory of Open Systems in Physics and Biology," *Science*,
111 (1950), pp. 23-29.

[16] Frequently in this chapter non-organismic examples are cited. This is done only when
they offer a more apt illustration of the phenomenon being described. It is assumed, further,
that they have their counterparts in living organisms, in each case.

[17] W. Köhler, *The Place of Value in a World of Facts* (New York: Liveright, 1938).

[18] Allport, "Theories of Perception," p. 472.

[19] H. G. Bray and K. White, "Organisms as Physico-Chemical Machines," *New Biology*, 16
(1954), p. 75.

In closed systems the final state is unequivocally determined by the initial conditions: for example, the motion of a planetary system where the position of the planets at a time t are unequivocally determined by their position at a time t_0. Or in a chemical equilibrium, the final concentrations of the reactants naturally depend on the initial concentrations. If either the initial conditions or the process is altered, the final state will also be changed. This is not so in open systems. Here the same final state may be reached from different initial conditions and in different ways. This is what is called equifinality, and it has a significant meaning for the phenomena of biological regulation. . . . The same final result, a normal individual of the sea urchin, can develop from a complete ovum, from each half of a divided ovum, or from the fusion product of two whole ova. The same applies to embryos of many other species, including man, where identical twins are the product of the splitting of one ovum.[20]

The phenomenon of equifinality in the human species may be illustrated by the case of two babies born at the same time, one of whom is premature, the other full-term. While at birth they will have been very different in appearance and stage of development, within a very few weeks after birth they will probably have achieved a similar stage of development. What this seems to mean is that for every species there is a typical or characteristic state; indeed, for every individual within the species there is a characteristic state which he, by nature, must strive to assume. It is perhaps more accurate to say he has characteristic states for each successive stage of development. At any given stage he strives to achieve and maintain a steady state around that which characterizes him— that which it is his nature to be at that stage in his development.

The concept of equifinality is very important in social work theory, particularly a theory based upon the philosophy enunciated earlier in this formulation. It was suggested that it is of the nature of human beings to be creators. On the basis of equifinality it follows that humans, regardless of their experiences, will strive to maintain a steady state around a condition that permits and fosters creativity. It is true, of course, that the price of maintaining such a steady state sometimes is so great that the individual gives up the struggle and we witness either his death or some form of human aberration. It is normal, nevertheless, for humans to be creators. Humans, by nature, are not content merely to adjust to their environment. They have an inner compulsion to influence it and shape it in ways that create ever more complex relationships between themselves and their environment.

Mention was made earlier of the competing processes of de-organization (entropy) and organization (negative entropy). Both operate in a living system during the entire course of its life. In the early stages of life, organization outruns de-organization, so that the organism becomes more and more differentiated or in other words it grows. With adulthood, life continues but growth slows to a stop. With old age de-organization outruns organization, and with death organization terminates and de-organization, resulting from the free play of entropy, has full reign.[21] While, admittedly, this is an over-simplified view of the aging process and needs to be supplemented by the inclusion of many other factors which surely must also operate, these comments by Bray and White, nevertheless, are of considerable relevance to social work theory. These writers make a further interesting observation to the effect that:

[20] Bertalanffy, "General Systems Theory," p. 77.
[21] Bray and White, "Organisms as Physico-Chemical Machines," p. 81.

All organisms live within an "astronomical" time scale which takes as its units external events. It is clear that there are other ways of considering the experience of time. For example, organisms compress within their life span the phases of growth, maturity, senescence. Herein lies the basis of a "biological" time scale. Du Nouy's observations led him to conclude that wound healing takes place as if astronomical time passed five times as quickly for a man of sixty as for a child of ten. This point of view is clearly related to what we may call the "subjective" time scale. It is almost proverbial that time seems to pass more and more rapidly as an individual grows older. This is manifest also in the fact that the movements and reactions of an aging individual appear to an observer to become slower and slower, while the person feels that the passage of external events is being accelerated. It is reasonable to suggest that the "subjective" and "biological" time scales are identical.[22]

Subjective and biological time scales are based on the rate of metabolism, and both are based on a thermodynamic time scale which, in turn, is based on the rate of entropy production.

Two additional phenomena remain to be described in the final section of this discussion of the properties of open systems. One is the dynamic interplay of processes and the other is the phenomenon of feedback. The steady state of an open system is maintained in part by the *dynamic interplay of its sub-systems operating as functional processes.* Each sub-system has its function or functions to perform, and it does so in relation to all of the others. This is the condition in a social system which Radcliffe-Brown has called *functional unity* and has defined as a condition in which all the parts of the social system work together with a sufficient degree of harmony or internal consistency, that is, without producing persistent conflicts which can neither be resolved nor regulated.[23]

The open system can also be maintained in or near a steady state by feedback processes.[24] Thermo-regulation in warm-blooded animals is one of the best examples of this process in living organisms. Cooling of the blood stimulates certain centres in the brain which "turn on" heat-producing mechanisms of the body, and the body temperature is monitored back to the centre so that temperature is maintained at a constant level. Bertalanffy gives several other examples of the feedback phenomenon,[25] one of which is Wiener's oft-quoted example of an individual in the process of picking up a pencil.[26] Report is made to the central nervous system of the extent to which one is moving toward the pencil in the first instance; this information is then fed back to the central nervous system so that the motion is controlled until it reaches its aim. Bertalanffy uses the following diagram to explain the stimulus-response sequence which occurs:

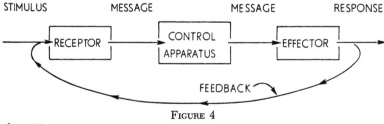

FIGURE 4

[22] *Ibid.,* p. 83.

[23] A. R. Radcliffe-Brown, "On the Concept of Function in Social Science," *American Anthropologist* (New Series), 37 (1935), p. 397.

[24] The author is indebted to Virginia Carlson of the 1957 Berkeley research group for her excellent analysis and application of the feedback concept.

[25] Bertalanffy, "General Systems Theory," p. 78.

[26] Norbert Wiener, *Cybernetics* (New York: John Wiley and Sons, 1948).

In feedback, the result of the effector's activity is monitored back so that the system is self-regulating.

The following definitions of feedback add one or more dimensions to our understanding of the concept. According to Wiener

Feedback is the property of being able to adjust future conduct by past performance. It may be simple as the common reflex, or it may be a higher order feedback, in which past experience is used not only to regulate specific movements, but also whole policies of behavior. Such a policy-feedback may, and often does, appear to be what we know under one aspect as a conditioned reflex, and under another as learning.[27]

And Hall and Fagen state that

Certain systems have the property that a portion of their outputs or behavior is fed back to the input and affects succeeding outputs. ... It is a well known fact that the nature, polarity and degree of feedback in a system have a decisive effect on the stability or instability of the system.[28]

Allport[29] has suggested that it is useful when considering such a feedback phenomenon to note that there is always a *mainline* function to which the feedback process is attached; specifically, this would be maintaining a constant body temperature or picking up a pencil in the examples cited.

Because each of the above are examples of *negative* feedback, it is important to note that feedback can also be *positive*. Such would be the case if a thermostat were constructed to supply more and more fuel the hotter the house became. This device, obviously, would not be used in house heating, but it is precisely the device that is used in space rockets which are specifically designed not to reach their maximum speed all at once.

Furthermore, there is *amplification* feedback which operates in both negative and positive feedback and wherein energy is both derivative and redirected. That is, no energy arises from the local source, but instead an additional source of energy is exploited and utilized in some particular way. Any chain reaction mechanism is an illustration of this phenomenon. For example, in uranium bombs a neutron splits an atomic nucleus which releases energy and more neutrons which split more atomic nuclei and release more energy. Another example, in the area of economics, is the inflationary spiral of increased wages leading to increased prices, leading to increased wages. Wisdom[30] has suggested that it is always important in referring to feedback mechanisms to indicate what type is involved in each case. It may be simple positive or negative feedback; it may be amplification feedback; or it may be mixed feedback. Furthermore, Virginia Carlson in her application of the feedback concept for purposes of explaining the dynamics of a riot situation in a correctional institution found it helpful to distinguish different kinds of feedback control systems.[31] There was the *intermittent* system where the monitoring took place at certain intervals of

---

[27] Norbert Wiener, *The Human Use of Human Beings* (New York: Doubleday Anchor Books, 1954), p. 33.

[28] Hall and Fagen, "Definition of System," p. 23.

[29] Allport, *Theories of Perception*, p. 522.

[30] J. O. Wisdom, "The Hypothesis of Cybernetics," *British Journal for the Philosophy of Science*, 2 (1951), pp. 1-24.

[31] V. Carlson *et al.*, "Social Work and General Systems Theory" (unpublished group research project, School of Social Welfare, University of California, Berkeley, 1957), pp. 83-104.

time. There was the *continuous* type in which the controlled quantity was continuously monitored. There was the *proportional* type which developed a correcting effort in proportion to the magnitude of difference between the required and the actual value of the controlled quantity. And there was the *relay* type of control, in which there were only two magnitudes, "on" and "off."

It is worth noting, too, as Wisdom has done,[32] that it is characteristic of regulatory mechanisms, both of the feedback and of the dynamic type, that the state of adaptation to the environment is only a hypothetical level around which the actual adjustment fluctuates. Thus, in a house with the thermostat set at seventy degrees, the temperature is almost never exactly seventy degrees, but varies above and below that reading. In other words, in an open system, changes occur in the environment causing successive compensations within the system. Hence, it describes a constant cyclical movement, the amplitude of the cycle being a function of the sensitivity of the mechanism. Sometimes a badly designed feedback mechanism over-compensates for environmental changes, thereby causing a series of increasingly wide oscillations. In machines this phenomenon is termed *dampened* feedback; in human beings it is associated with certain kinds of injury to the cerebellum.[33]

Finally, another of Bertalanffy's observations concerning the relation between feedback and the dynamic interplay of processes has particular relevance to theory of social work practice, particularly theory conceived in the terms of this formulation. He says:

It should be borne in mind, however, that the feedback scheme is of a rather special nature. It presupposes structural arrangements of the type mentioned [in the typical stimulus-response sequence]. There are, however, many regulations in the living organism which are of essentially different nature, namely, those where the order is effectuated by a dynamic interplay of processes. Remember the classical example of embryonic regulation where the whole is re-established from the parts in an equifinal process. It can be shown that the *primary* regulation in organic systems, that is, those which are most fundamental and primitive in embryonic development as well as in evolution, are of such nature of dynamic interaction. They are based upon the fact that the living organism is an open system, maintaining itself in, or approaching a steady state. Superimposed are those regulations which may be called *secondary*, and which are controlled by fixed arrangements, especially of the feedback type. This state of affairs is in consequence of a general principle of organization which may be called progressive mechanization. At first, systems—biological, neurological, psychological or social—are governed by dynamic interaction of their components; later on, fixed arrangements and conditions of constraint are established which render the system and its parts more efficient, but also gradually diminish and eventually abolish its equipotentiality. Thus, dynamics is the broader aspect, since we can always arrive from general systems laws to machine-like function by introducing suitable conditions of constraint, but the opposite way is not practicable.[34]

With the concepts which have been introduced so far it is possible to describe in general the manner and extent to which an organism is able to maintain itself in a steady state. Possibly a summary of what has been said in this regard may be useful, however, at this point.

There is a dynamic interplay among the essential functional sub-processes or sub-systems in the organismic system which enables it to maintain itself in a

---

[32] Wisdom, "The Hypothesis of Cybernetics."

[33] The author is indebted for this and a number of other useful references to Mrs. Hanna Pitkin, University of California, Berkeley.

[34] Bertalanffy, "General Systems Theory," p. 79.

homeostatic steady state. Assuming a sufficient input of material from its environment, the organism develops toward a characteristic state despite initial conditions (equifinality). All of this is accomplished through an automatic self-regulatory process.

In addition, however, and concurrently, certain other processes are developing which impose limitations upon this natural regulatory process. A process occurs, for instance, which Bertalanffy calls *progressive segregation*,[35] wherein the system divides into a hierarchial order of subordinate systems which gain a certain independence of each other. An extreme case, he points out, is a tumor which behaves as if it were an independent organism, and thus destroys the whole of which it is a part. Another example which he cites, of the normal operation of progressive segregation, is the case of patients recovering after cerebral injuries. "It is not punctual sensations which reappear first. A point-light causes, at first, not the sensation of a luminous point, but of a vaguely circumscribed brightness; only later on, perception of shapes and finally of points is restored. Similar to embryonic development, the restoration of vision progresses from an undifferentiated to a differentiated state, and the same probably holds true for the phylogenetic evolution of perception."[36] It has been assumed in this formulation that this process of progressive segregation is related to what was referred to earlier as the production of negative entropy, wherein there is progression to higher levels of order and differentiation. Accompanying the process of progressive segregation is that of *progressive mechanization*, wherein certain processes become set as fixed arrangements. Examples are the various feedback mechanisms that have already been described.

There are two consequences of the operation of these two processes. One is that the entropic forces, the forces toward de-differentiation and homogeneity, are held in check, that is, progressive mechanization and segregation are life-maintaining. The other is that they impose constraints upon the free interplay of the functional sub-systems of the system, in which case they would seem to impose a limit upon the degree to which the system may achieve its potentiality.

All this would seem to be particularly relevant to a theory of social work practice based as it is upon the idea that human beings are continually in a state of approaching, but never reaching, their full potentiality. The fact that the fixing of arrangements, the imposing of constraints, while a necessary condition of organization, limits the extent to which the organism may realize its potentiality, is perhaps at the basis of the social work principles of maximizing self-regulation and self-determination and of keeping manipulation by external agents to a minimum.

Finally, because social work is concerned with the organism especially when it is under stress or when normal regulatory processes have broken down, it may be useful to refer in a general way to the various pathological conditions which may develop in organismic systems. Reference has already been made to the possible faulty operation of feedback mechanisms. In addition, it is also possible

[35] Bertalanffy, "An Outline of General Systems Theory," p. 148.
[36] Ludwig von Bertalanffy, "Theoretical Models in Biology and Psychology," *Journal of Personality*, 20 (1951), p. 28.

that the input of essential energy and material may be so inadequate that the system is unable to maintain a steady state (the candle goes out when its food supply is exhausted). This is the case of all living organisms which are denied at least the minimum of life essentials. A special condition would be that in which there is an abundance of energy and material but it is in the wrong form or state to enable the system to utilize it. Another pathological condition may arise from the inadequate operation of one or more of the essential functional sub-parts of the system. A group, for instance, might falter and even be forced out of existence for lack of an adequate communication system among its members. Or, there may be adverse conditions arising from the unsuccessful attempt of the system to establish a new steady state. Burton has shown that there is always some cost in energy as a result of the transition to a new steady state.[37] Resources are usually adequate to pay any such cost of transition, but, Burton points out, it is a peculiarity of open systems, whose reactants are combined by catalytic processes, that sometimes the cost of transition to new steady state exceeds that *threshold* of the system and it departs temporarily or permanently from its steady state. Such a departure, of course, is not only pathological but, if permanent, is also fatal to the system.

Organismic Systems in Terms of Structure, Function, and Process

Most of what has been said up to this point about systems in general, and organismic systems in particular, has been drawn from physical and biological theory. Now it should be fully acknowledged that the sociologists and cultural anthropologists have also made effective use of the concept. Talcott Parsons and others have developed a theory of *social systems* which they define as a system of interactive relationships of a plurality of individual actors.[38] A society, in their terms, is not only a social system but also a very complex network of interlocking and interdependent sub-systems, each of which is equally authentically a social system. Groups, communities, and societies are essentially open living systems, or they are, in Parsons' terms, social systems.

Similarly, there are many anthropological concepts which seem to correspond to the systems model. Radcliffe-Brown, for instance, holds that a comprehensive view of the living organism, whether it be an individual, group, or society, must be conceived in terms of its structure, function, and process.[39] The individual human organism has life—an on-going *process*. The arrangement of its tissues, organs, and fluids is its *structure*. The connection between the life process and the structure of the organism is its *function*. The series of processes which occur in living are dependent on the organic structure. The link is function. Thus, the heart, for example, a part of the structure, has the function of pumping blood. So long as it continues to carry on its function, the life process goes on. If it

[37] A. C. Burton, "The Properties of the Steady State Compared to Those of Equilibrium as Shown in Characteristic Biological Behavior," *Journal of Cellular and Comparative Physiology*, 14 (1939), pp. 327-349.

[38] T. Parsons and E. A. Shils, *Toward a General Theory of Action* (Cambridge, Mass.: Harvard University Press, 1951).

[39] A. R. Radcliffe-Brown, *Structure and Function in Primitive Society* (Glencoe, Ill.: Free Press, 1952).

ceases, the process stops. Process and structure, therefore, are mutually dependent.

At the level of the social system, whether it be group, community, or society, the same analysis is possible. A social sytem consists of persons arranged in some ordered fashion. The arrangement is the *social structure*. Social process and social structure are linked by function. Thus, if we wish to understand some aspect of social life, we have to determine the connection between structural features and the social process.[40]

While considering these concepts of process, structure, and function it may be of some interest to note, parenthetically, that the social work profession has tried to clarify social work operations first by process or method, everything coming under casework, group work, or community organization. Then we tried classification according to structure, with services under child welfare auspices, services under public assistance auspices, and so forth. And now we are moving toward the classification of services in terms of function—what the service purports to do.

Finally, then, the high degree of correspondence between the concept of social systems or the manner of conceiving human organization in terms of structure, function, and process and the way in which the biologists and psychologists, in particular, have conceived them, as open organismic systems, should be apparent. Open organismic systems and their sub-systems have structure; they also have function. And the dynamic interplay of the sub-systems, in maintaining the total system in a steady state, can validly be regarded as process.

This rather extended discussion of the systems construct has been presented largely in the terms used by the general systems theorists. In the next chapter, consideration is given to the extent to which the organismic form of the systems construct coincides with the philosophical position advanced in this formation; and the construct is evaluated to determine whether it is likely to provide an adequate means around which to organize a common conceptual framework for representing the social work client—whether that client be an individual, a group, a community, or some continuous complex of all three.

---

[40] The author is indebted to Professor Morton Teicher, Director, Department of Social Work, Yeshiva University, New York City, among other useful suggestions, for this elaboration of Radcliffe-Brown's theory.

Chapter VI

JUSTIFICATION, EVALUATION, MODIFICATION

The power of any conceptual framework to generate pregnant theory depends in large part upon an appropriate choice of central integrating construct. A construct that is well chosen will be consistent with the theory builder's value-orientation and capable of comprehending and accurately representing the realities which constitute the theory domain. Up to this point in the present discussion a philosophical base has been defined and *organismic system* has been introduced as the central integrating construct. The purpose of this chapter, then, is to evaluate and justify the choice, and to indicate some modifications which might possibly increase the integrating and theory-generating power of the construct.

JUSTIFICATION

System of the organismic type was chosen as the central integrating construct because it seemed directly related in so many ways to the values and beliefs underlying this formulation. The reader will recall that the larger project, of which this is a part, is the quest for a basis upon which to formulate a particular conception of the social work process—a conception which regards casework, group work, and community organization as aspects of a single unified process. It holds that if individuals, groups, and communities can all be regarded as systems, and if there are certain properties common to them all, it seems likely that there may also be certain common principles that define their operation and that the latter may form a part, at least, of a unified conception of social work. This form of the systems construct seems to provide a means, as well, of representing particular individuals—in groups—in communities—as a single dynamic complex; such a representation, if successful, would provide an even greater hope for the development of a unified view of the social work process.

The concept of open organismic system, exchanging material and energy continually with its environment, seems to be a particularly apt way of representing individuals, groups, and communities. Numerous direct parallels may be cited between the way in which organismic systems function and the way in which people function as individuals, or in groups and communities. Just as man, for instance, has been described as a creator, so do organismic systems, characteristically, create higher forms of organization out of the free energy and material which they draw from the environment. Man is continually approaching the state which characterizes his species; organismic systems tend to move toward a similar state from different initial conditions. Man is capable of achieving and maintaining a homeostatic state; organismic systems, by means of feedback and the dynamic interplay of constituent processes, are able to maintain themselves in a steady state. Just as man is never quite the same at any successive stage of development, for as Heraclitus and others have said, he can never return to a *status quo ante*, so we observe that organismic systems are for the most part irreversible and tend to go in one direction only in the course of their development.[1]

Similarly, other implications derived from the systems construct have seemed entirely consistent with the values upon which this view of the social work process is based. Just as social workers try to help clients develop an optimum degree of individuality amid counter social pressures to conformity, so, in organismic systems, there is the tendency to establish fixed arrangements which, if they become too numerous or too strong may seriously hamper the natural dynamic interplay of processes which maintains the organismic system in a steady state. The social worker tries to prevent or alleviate the socially or psychologically damaging effects of crisis situations; there are crises which can develop out of any one of a number of pathological conditions in organismic systems. The social worker comes into relationship from out of the client's distal environment when a need for service arises, and goes back, not into the distal but into the proximal environment when his function has been served. That is, he is "out" of the client's life although available should need for service arise again. The social worker tries to help the client develop self-insight which, in systemic terms, would mean that the worker tries to help the client, as a system, to become aware of the condition around which it ought to be trying to maintain a steady state, and he tries, further, to help the client develop an awareness of what is impeding and what is promoting the attainment of that steady state.

It is important, however, to recognize fully the fact that systems are amoral. That is, the systemic framework will serve just as well to represent the objects for which a charlatan or an unscrupulous manipulator might operate as it will for those of the social worker. This fact, however, should in no way disqualify the use of the systems construct in social work theory. It simply means that social workers must specify certain values to regulate their manner of functioning and their purpose for working within the complex as represented.

These direct parallels between the construct of organismic system and certain values and beliefs seem to provide ample justification for its use as the integrating device for the present theory domain, although it is acknowledged, of course, that the ultimate decision as to the adequacy of the system construct must also depend in part upon an evaluation of what the construct can or cannot contribute to social work theory building and to social work practice.

EVALUATION

Some strengths

The greatest strength of the systems construct resides in the fact that the meanings attached to it seem, with one or two exceptions which will be noted

[1] The author is indebted for this suggestion to Professor Olive M. Stone, School of Social Welfare, University of California, Los Angeles.

later, entirely consistent with the values and beliefs upon which this formulation is based. Furthermore, the construct seems to be capable, eventually if not immediately, of providing a good framework within which to conceive the social work process.

Some limitations

The limitations in the systems construct as herein described seem to be faults of both omission and inclusion. Its failure in certain instances, for example, stems from the fact that it provides only a partial picture of the complex in which social work occurs. In another instance, the construct seems to convey a somewhat misleading idea of the nature and functioning of individuals, groups, and communities.

The tendency of open systems to develop from various beginnings to a condition which is fairly common for the species, and then to maintain themselves in a steady state around that particular condition, has been correctly and fully established; however, the construct does little to indicate what that final condition is destined to be. This, of course, is a rather serious limitation in social work, since in order to perform its proper function, its workers must have a clear idea of what is normal growth and a healthy state of being. And man is a purposive being, that is, whether he is functioning alone or with his fellows in groups or communities, there is purpose in his behaviour. The systems construct does not seem to deal very adequately with this fact of man's nature.

General systems theory tells us that open systems maintain themselves in steady states through the operation of feedback mechanisms and the dynamic interplay of processes. The theory does not tell us, however, what these mechanisms or processes may be or how they operate in relation to one another in individuals, groups, and communities. Similarly, while general systems theory holds that individuals, groups, and communities may each be regarded as open organismic systems, it does not indicate very clearly how individuals—in groups —in communities—form a complex which may also function as an open organismic system. In the case of this larger complex, what are the sub-systems, for instance, which presumably are functioning within the system?

Another possible limitation in the utility of the systems construct for social work theory stems from its necessarily high level of abstraction. It is so abstract that the practitioner finds it difficult to apply whatever insights may be derived from it. The proposition, for instance, that all groups have boundaries, structure, functional sub-systems, and so on, has the virtue of being universal, but the vice of failing to answer the questions that worry practitioners who need to know what kind of structure is most likely to contribute to maximizing the therapy potential, the recreation potential, or the decision-making potential of the group.[2] This high level of abstraction, however, becomes an impediment only if the theory building process stops at the conceptualizing phase. One need only take

[2] The author is indebted to Professor Joseph W. Eaton, Lecturer in Social Welfare, University of California, Los Angeles, for this observation about a potential limitation in the use of the systems construct.

the next step which is to concretize or elaborate the practical implication of the theory derived from the abstract construct, to overcome this limitation.

One possible source of error arises from having regarded open and closed systems as if they operated in a pure or perfect form, and organismic systems as if they were completely open systems. Such, of course, is never the case, for there is no system which is perfectly closed in the sense of being completely independent of its environment. And there is no system which, in all areas and at all times, is completely open. Frequently, certain areas of "open" systems become somewhat isolated from the whole and thus tend to function more like closed systems. This problem of openness-closedness is discussed further in the following section of this chapter in which certain modifications are proposed.

First, on the basis of this evaluation we may conclude that the systems construct as herein described is consistent with the values and beliefs which were defined and, with certain modifications, will serve adequately as a general overall framework for conceptualizing the complex in which social work occurs. It is true that many other concepts will have to be devised within the organismic systems construct in order to make the representation more complete. Appropriate analogues will be required to make more apparent the operation of organismic systems. Finally, some more adequate way will have to be found to deal with the open and closed nature of organismic systems.

MODIFICATIONS

There are two ideas which have not been incorporated into the present formulation despite the fact they occupy a fairly important position in general systems literature. The reason they have not been included here is that they appear to be inconsistent with certain crucial aspects of the philosophical position underlying this formulation.

The first of these ideas is contained in an observation by Floyd Allport to the effect that all "open" systems are ultimately closed. In discussing the candle flame which he used as an illustration of the maintenance of a steady state, he says:

If we consider the burning candle and the surrounding atmosphere as a larger unlimited (but therefore "closed") system we see that the potential energy of the whole system (as stored in the candle subsystem) is continually being reduced. An equilibrium with the surroundings would therefore be ultimately attained (second law of thermodynamics) unless the store of food in the candle could be continually replaced. However, since the flame of the candle is the only way in which the potential energy reduction can take place, the system will lose its potential energy the more quickly the more of it passes into the flame. For this reason the flame contains continually a maximum of potential energy. . . . we could say that in order to achieve the energy dissipation required by thermodynamical principles the working part of the entire system that is provided by the open system of the candle maintains a steady condition that seems opposed to the law. It seems opposed, however, only while we are considering it within its own confines or region. This situation is also typical of living organisms. They remain in steady states, but only so long as a food supply is available.[3]

William F. Line suggests that this means that ultimately there is only one system,

[3] Floyd H Allport, *Theories of Perception and the Concept of Structure* (New York: John Wiley and Sons, 1955), p. 472.

the universe, and that, obviously, it is closed.[4] Having taken the opposite view we must disagree, in this instance, both with Allport and with Line. Having identified ourselves with those who believe in the continuous creation of an expanding universe, we must take the position that the universe is essentially open. We would agree with Allport that systems can only remain in steady states as long as a food supply is available. But having assumed that the universe is continuously expanding, we must further assume that the supply *will* always be available. Similarly, we cannot hold with those who have predicted the ultimate heat death of the universe (cf. p. 41) for the same philosophical reasons.

Another idea which we have not been able to accept completely is James Miller's suggestion that the modern electronic computer may serve as the analogue of an open system of the organismic type. It may be appropriate in the case of certain types of open systems, but it seems quite inappropriate in the case of the organismic system. While such man-made machines do have remarkable similarities to living organismic systems, there are also marked dissimilarities. The manner in which machines incorporate energy and information is different from that of organisms; energy and information in machines come from an outside source rather than, in part, from within the system; they do not regenerate damaged parts; they do not resist unanticipated disruption to their steady state; and they are incapable of reproducing their kind. The machine analogue, as was indicated earlier, may be usefully and appropriately employed, however, to represent certain of the fixed arrangements of the feedback type which organisms develop in the process of progressive mechanization.

An Alternate Analogue for Organismic Systems

Another analogue which is more attractive to us (perhaps because it is more consistent with our philosophical position), is one suggested by Floyd Allport.[5] It is a part of his new approach to perception theory. He believe that it is incorrect to represent organismic systems as linear processes of the machine type with input and output between themselves and their environment. Systems, he believes, always operate as self-closing, circular processes. Individuals, groups, or communities are actually complex circular structures of many interrelated circular processes. This, of course, is what is implied in the idea of the dynamic interplay of processes which help to maintain systems in steady states. Allport also represents all feedback mechanisms as circular processes attached to particular mainline circular processes. He believes that, ultimately, it may be possible to state the laws which regulate the operations of these complexes which he has chosen to call *event-structures*. His scheme is only in its earliest stage of development, of course, but already would seem to hold great promise for the further extension of general systems theory, particularly that part which is concerned with organismic systems.

[4] While disagreeing with Professor Line of the University of Toronto in this instance, the author is indebted to him in a great many ways for his interest, his encouragement, and his many helpful suggestions.

[5] Floyd H. Allport, *Theories of Perception*, chap. xxi and "The Structuring of Events: Outline of a General Theory with Applications to Psychology," *Psychological Review*, 61 (1954), pp. 281-303.

The Characteristic State of an Organism

One of the more serious limitations of the present formulation is that while it postulates the idea of an organism maintaining itself in a steady state, it does not suggest what may be the characteristic state for an organism at any given stage of its development. One cannot help but feel that the means are available, however, and that in time this particular inadequacy will be fairly easily overcome. Erik Erikson's theoretical formulations, for instance, might be usefully employed to this end.[6] He has provided an important interpretation and extension of Bertalanffy's concept of equifinality in his diagram of the "eight stages" through which the individual as a result of his interaction with others moves as he integrates what Erikson calls the organ modes with the moral and social modes. There are also various formulations available to account for the energy which organismic systems are able to generate. As a final example, a concept of the developing self as a process of "becoming," after the order of a recent formulation by Gordon Allport,[7] might also be usefully employed.

Openness and Closedness of Organismic Systems

The question of whether a system is ever open or closed can perhaps best be settled by assuming that it is both—that is, at any given time a system, and especially an organismic system, possesses some degree of both openness and closedness. Certain of an organism's sub-sytems, for instance, might function at certain times as closed systems while the rest were functioning as open systems. Certainly this is a most apt way of describing the schizophrenic individual or a group such as the Hutterites referred to earlier (cf. p. 40). And it seems very likely that all other living systems may be similar in kind although not in degree to these two examples.

One might postulate as another characteristic of organismic systems the fact that their openness is only temporary and transitory. A system may eventually die, and when it does it will, of course, cease to exist as an organismic system and will assume what has been characterized as the final state of a closed system. Negative entropy will cease and positive entropy will have full reign. Such a reformulation around the idea of organismic systems in no way diminishes the importance of the earlier descriptions of open and closed systems. These concepts still serve the useful purpose of defining the manner in which the open and closed aspects of the organismic systems can be expected to function.

There are some additional questions for which general systems literature does not yet appear to supply ready answers. What, for instance, are the functional sub-systems of groups and communities? How are they interrelated as a dynamic whole? Some speculations concerning these questions will be offered in the final chapter.

To summarize the discussion to this point, justification has been offered for the choice of the organismic construct as a logical derivative from the stated philosophical position of this formulation. This construct, as conceived by the

---

[6] Erik H. Erikson, *Childhood and Society* (New York: W. W. Norton, 1950), chap. VII.
[7] Gordon W. Allport, *Becoming* (New Haven: Yale University Press, 1955), chap. XI.

general systems theorists, has proved satisfactory in certain respects, although somewhat inadequate in others, as a means of representing the various clients with whom the social work process deals. Certain possible modifications designed to increase its adequacy have been proposed, leading us, as the final matter for consideration, to the determination of the ways that the systems construct, as modified, can and should be applied toward the extension of social work theory.

Chapter VII

PROMISE AWAITING FULFILMENT

Kurt Lewin's oft-quoted observation that there is nothing as practical as a good theory suggests, conversely, that one way to estimate the quality of theory is to determine its practicality. What new ideas, if any, does it suggest? What new research hypotheses does it raise? What new patterns for practice does it indicate? This final chapter suggests some possible contributions to social work theory which it seems reasonable to expect might accrue from the employment of general systems theory. As this monograph is written, it must be acknowledged, however, that these are but potential contributions, the actual utility of which has as yet been only partially demonstrated. The final sections, consequently, also describe some of the specific and immediate tasks which will have to be undertaken, first to demonstrate, and then to utilize, the theory-generating potential of the general systems approach.

THE PROMISE

It has been the contention of this monograph that individuals, groups, and communities can all be represented as organismic systems, since each appears to manifest, in one form or another, all the properties of such systems. Further, it has been claimed that general systems theory can be used as a basis upon which to build a generic theory of social work practice. It is time, now, to elaborate upon these claims and to see what evidence can be mustered in their support.

COMMON REPRESENTATION OF ORGANISMIC SYSTEMS

The crucial test of the first claim is whether, in fact, it is possible to define a common set of dimensions capable, at once, of describing the structure and functioning of individuals, groups, and communities. Table I, together with the description which follows, represents such an attempt in that it suggests several general aspects of organismic systems and describes the particular form which they assume in the case of individuals, groups, and communities.

Structural Components

The various organs of the body, the psychological processes, and in particular their arrangement in relation to one another constitute the structure of the individual. To conceive and represent the comparable structural components of groups, however, it is necessary to introduce and define the concepts *status* and *role.* Linton has defined status as "the place in a particular system which a certain individual occupies at a particular time with respect to that system."[1] All statutes in that system, regarded collectively, may be designated as a *status system*. Actually, there are many such status systems in any group, the totality of which may be regarded as the *status structure* of the group. Similarly, role is defined as "the sum total of cultural patterns associated with a particular status. It thus includes attitudes, values, and behaviour ascribed by the society to any and all persons occupying this status. Role is the dynamic aspect of status; what the individual has to do in order to validate his occupation of the status."[2] As in the case of status, it is possible to identify *role systems* and a total *role structure*.

TABLE I

REPRESENTATION OF INDIVIDUALS, GROUPS AND COMMUNITIES ALONG COMMON DIMENSIONS

System	Structural Components	Sub-systems° °The structural components arranged and operating to perform the functions essential to the organism	System variables † † Factors affecting systems through functioning of sub-systems	Environment	Environmental parameters ‡ ‡ Factors determining the nature of the environment
Individual	Cells	Circulatory, excretory, respiratory, procreational, etc. (organs and their extensions)	Age, health, maturity, degree of personality integration, etc.	Everything external to the boundary of the individual	Ecological, social, climatic, cultural, historical, etc.
Group	Individuals in terms of their statuses and roles	Communication evaluation, executive control, boundary maintenance, etc. (social processes)	Size, maturity of members, degree of institutionalization, etc.	Everything external to the boundary of the group	Ecological, social, climatic, cultural, historical, etc.
Community Constellation	Individuals, organizations and groups in terms of their statuses and roles	Communication evaluation, executive control, boundary maintenance, etc. (social processes)	Number of interlocking groups and individuals, diversity of individual and group ideologies, etc.	Everything external to the boundary of the community	Ecological, social, climatic, cultural, historical, etc.

---

[1] Ralph Linton, *The Concept of Role and Status—The Cultural Background of Personality* (New York: D. Appleton-Century Co., Inc., 1945), p. 76.

[2] *Ibid.*, p. 77.

It is the latter in combination with the status structure, which constitutes the general structural dimension of the group.

In the case of communities it is much the same except that in groups statuses are occupied and roles are played by individuals, whereas in communities statuses are occupied and roles are played by individuals and by constituent groups and organizations.

This is the first reference to organizations. In subsequent formulations it seems clear that organizations or agencies can and should also be regarded as systems. In a recent book by Lippitt, Watson, and Westley on the process of planned change, the authors refer to individuals, groups, organizations, and communities as client-systems and indicate that structurally and functionally similar problems occur in each and that the process of facilitating planned change in each is essentially the same.[3] It seems clear that an adequate representation of the community as an organismic system would require such conceptualization of agencies or organizations as systems because they, with individuals and groups, are the structural components of communities.[4]

It seems clear also that "community" will always have to be defined separately and differentially in relation to each successive welfare problem. Part of the job of the community organization worker, after a proper diagnosis of the problem, is to define the "community" for the particular health and welfare problem at hand. An adoption problem, for instance, will have a particular constellation of groups, social organizations, and individuals and, hence, a particular structure. A problem concerning neighbourhood recreation presumably would have different organizations, groups, and individuals. There would also be times, of course, when one would be concerned with the total geographic community as an integrated, balanced, and functioning organism. Such would be the case, for instance, where a community was mobilizing itself during a flood, fire, or similar threat to its existence.

While fully acknowledging the fact that organizations can, should, and in fact have, also been represented as organismic systems,[5] for the sake of simplicity this is not done in the present formulation but has been indicated as one of the tasks for the future.

Sub-systems

At all three levels, the sub-systems comprise all of those functional processes upon which the life and continued existence of the organism depends. In the individual they consist of the various physiological and psychological systems: circulatory, digestive, excretory, respiratory, motivational, perceptive, and so on. In the group and community, the sub-systems include the similar processes by which the group or community attempts to maintain itself in a steady state.

---

[3] Ronald Lippitt, Jeanne Watson, and Bruce Westley, *The Dynamics of Planned Change: A Comparative study of Principles and Techniques* (New York: Harcourt, Brace and Company, 1957).

[4] The author is again indebted to Genevieve Carter for a number of helpful suggestions regarding the application of general systems theory to the representation of a community.

[5] R. Sorenson and H. S. Dimock, *Designing Education in Values* (New York: Association Press, 1955).

System Variables

As used here, a system variable is any measurable internal attribute which is assumed to affect a system or any of its sub-systems.[6] Thus, in the individual there might be included among the variables such attributes as age, health, maturity, personality integration, and so on; in the group, such factors as size, maturity of the members, extent of institutionalization, and so on; and in the community, such factors as the size of the interlocking network of individuals, organizations, and groups, the diversity among their various individual, group, and organizational value-orientations, and so on.

Environment

In each case the environment of a system—individual, group, or community—is everything that is external to its boundary. Higher levels of systems, as we have seen, are always a part of the environments of lower levels.

One might well ask at this point where social welfare as an institution, social agencies as part of the structure of social welfare, and the social worker as the agent, belong in this analysis. Are they to be regarded as a part of the environment, or as systems, or as structural components of systems? The best answer, probably, is that they may be all of these at different times. Social welfare, the institution, may certainly be regarded as a social system, but it may also be regarded as a part of the environment of the social agency, the client, and the worker, and it may be regarded as one of the structural components of the larger society. Similarly, the agency and the social worker can be perceived in these various contexts.

From the point of view of the client, also, the agency and the worker may seem to occupy various positions with respect to him. Taking casework as an example, the sequence of a typical relationship usually begins with the worker as part of the client's distal environment from which he usually moves fairly quickly into the proximal environment. As the relationship continues, however, the worker and client become welded, at least to some extent, into a dyadic system, manifesting all the characteristic properties of such. Later, in the termination process, the worker tries to move back into the proximal and ultimately into the client's distal environment. Social workers know how important it is for them to assess correctly where the client perceives them to be at various stages in the relationship and to capitalize fully upon these perceptions in the helping process.

Environmental Parameters

A comprehensive scheme for representing the many facets of the environment will have to be developed, ultimately, in a total formulation. Let it suffice at this

---

[6] This usage is at variance with Miller (cf. James G. Miller, "Toward a General Theory for the Behavioral Sciences," *American Psychologist*, 10, 1955, p. 514) who defines a variable as "those specific functions of a system which we can stipulate and whose magnitude we can measure in a relative scale" and a sub-system as "any components of an organism that can affect a variable." We believe that the present distinction between structural components, sub-systems, and system variables provides somewhat more precision and greater clarity.

stage, however, to indicate that such a scheme will undoubtedly include, among others, the ecological, social, geographical, and historical aspects. With these facets identified, the environmental parameters may then be designated as the particular varying conditions of these facets.

Transformation of Reference Frames

What has been contended in this formulation is that it is possible to utilize the same phenomena, the same conceptual framework, and the same approach in representing the individual, group, organization, and community. P. G. Herbst, at the conclusion of an article in which he has employed the systems construct in relation to several levels of behaviour systems, says:

It has been shown that within any behavior system three types of forces operate on the components of the system; these are (a) forces deriving from the components, (b) forces deriving from the system, and (c) forces that have their source in the environment of the system. In the case of the individual these were seen to correspond to valence, internal pressure, and social pressure respectively. If we now take as our unit of analysis a group of which the individual is a member, then the individual who was previously looked at as a single system now takes on the role of a component within the behavior system of the group. The forces operating within the group with respect to its members as components will be (a) forces deriving from members, (b) forces deriving from the group as a system, and (c) forces having their source in the group's environment. These are clearly the same forces as we have been considering before only differentiated from one another in a different way.

In passing from the individual to the group as a unit of analysis, the joint component and system forces of the individual now become the component forces of the group, while the social pressures operating on the individual now become split off into the system forces of the group and those having their source in the environment of the group. If an institution is defined as a set of interdependent groups, then by a similar shift to the next higher unit of analysis we arrive at the forces operating on groups as components of an institution.

The transition from one unit of analysis to another within a hierarchy of behavior systems is seen to involve a change in frame of reference in the conceptual representation of behavior events, but not in the type of phenomena included in the analysis.[7]

A Group as an Organismic System

Having shown that living organisms such as the individual, the group, the organization, and the community may be represented as manifesting the several structural and functional properties of organismic systems, it may be useful at this point, by way of example, to describe one of these orders of organism in somewhat greater detail, using the concepts of general systems theory. Because it has been the author's principal focus of theoretical interest, the *group* has been chosen for elaboration.

In what sense do groups exist? Vladimir Cervinka has suggested that we may conceive of a group in two ways: (1) we may think of the physical group, the "real" group, composed of those persons whom we arbitrarily designate as composing the group; or (2) we may abstract for analysis any aspect of the interaction of the members.[8] For example, we might consider the phenomenon of the giving and taking of orders in a family. We would observe who in the family gives and takes orders from whom under different circumstances. If

[7] P. G. Herbst, "Situation Dynamics and the Theory of Behavior Systems," *Behavioral Science*, 2 (1957), p. 28.

[8] Vladimir Cervinka, "A Dimensional Theory of Groups," *Sociometry*, 11 (1948), pp. 100-107.

we abstracted and charted this phenomenon, we would have what Cervinka calls a *groupoid*. And of course we could develop groupoids for as many phenomena in the group as we chose to study, their value being their amenability to mathematical manipulation. With them we would be able to develop basic theory, to formulate hypotheses whose validity might then be tested in the real physical group.

It is our present view that individuals come together and interact and that in time their interactions assume a patterned quality. Patterning occurs in the sense that as time goes on the same individuals tend to interact for certain purposes in the same ways. These patterns tend to persist over time, even in some cases beyond the life span of the persons whose interactions initiated them. Furthermore, products or property, such as physical objects, ideas, and symbols, are often produced from the interaction among the members, and these, too, are included in our reference to the group.

Perhaps one may sum up the matter by agreeing with Cervinka that there are two ways of conceiving the group. There is the group composed of actual persons and there is also the abstraction we call the group (groupoid). In this latter sense *group*, like *system*, is a hypothetical construct. We act "as if" it actually existed.[9] We assume that the group functions as an organismic system in the sense that it exchanges material with its environment and strives to maintain a steady state. It develops sub-systems which perform the functions essential to its survival, and these sub-systems tend to achieve a functional unity.

The boundary of a group. It has already been suggested (cf. p. 42) that the boundary of a group can be defined in terms of the amount and intensity of interaction among its members. For example, measured by the manifestation of the exchange of energy and information in the group, the boundary of the group will be that region where there is a certain specified amount d less interpersonal interaction than there is outside that region or immediately inside it. Thus the boundary of a group is always an arbitrary designation.

The structure of a group. The maintenance of a system in a steady state requires a structure through which a number of sub-systems may function in an interrelated way. It has already been suggested (cf. p. 59) that individuals assume certain positions or statuses in the group and that certain prescribed behaviours (roles) are associated with these positions. Among these prescriptions are those which define the relationships that should exist between persons occupying the different positions in the group. Thus, for each of the many facets in the life of the group there are such status-role-relationship prescriptions, and these collectively constitute its structure.

The functioning of a group. Within such a structure the group functions through the interrelated operation of several sub-systems. But the place to begin any discussion of the functioning of a group is with the consideration of the *purpose* of the group and the function it serves. It is assumed here that all groups at any given time have a purpose even if, in some instances, it may

---

[9] The author is indebted to Dr. W. F. Hill, Utah State Hospital, for this suggestion.

be to "find a purpose." The purpose of the group partially defines the characteristic or proper state for that group and the condition around which it will attempt to maintain a steady state. Reference here is to the purpose *as the group itself perceives it.* It is important, of course, to realize that because there can be radical changes both in the group and in its environment, its purposes may change frequently during the course of its life. Presumably each major shift in purpose requires alterations in the structure of the group, a redefinition of the proper state and an attempted shift to a new steady state.

In the process of maintaining any steady state the group exchanges energy and information with its environment. *Energy,* like the other functional processes of the group, operates through the members. It may emanate from forces deriving from members, forces deriving from the group as a system, or forces having their source in the environment of the group. Similarly, *information* is carried by and expressed through members. It defines the relationships among persons and among things which the members have experienced.

What happens within the system? How does it use the energy and information it imports? What functional sub-systems must groups develop in order to maintain a steady state? This is a point, in particular, where the counsel of the phenomenologists should be taken seriously. They would say that one should not try to answer these questions except upon the subjective reports of the "systems" themselves concerning what occurs within them, or at least any *a priori* formulations should be tested in reality before being assigned an important position in one's conceptual framework.

In the present formulation we have assumed on the basis of observation and logical deduction that, in order for groups to exist as unitary organisms, such functions as the formulating of a group value system, the defining and maintaining of the group's boundary, the control and co-ordination of members' actions, the communication of intentions and desires among members, the distribution and redistribution of power to accomplish certain purposes, the receiving, coding and storing of information for future reference, to name but a few, must exist. The means by which each of these functions is accomplished might be regarded as a separate sub-system, all sub-systems functioning, nevertheless, in an interdependent relationship as a functional unity.

The variables of a group as a system. Probably the most useful way to conceive of the variables of a group is to think in terms of the factors that may affect the operation of any one or more of the functional sub-systems (once they are identified). The size of the group for example, might be regarded as one such variable. As the number of members increases, the means of maintaining the various functional sub-systems will likely become more complex and will probably require more fixed arrangements which in turn, as was noted earlier, will impose constraints upon the group, limiting its flexibility and spontaneity. Similarly, one could imagine how such factors as the length of time the group had been in existence, the age and maturity of its members, and its purpose might also affect the form and operation of the various sub-systems. One could enumerate an almost endless number of such variables and all would be important to the understanding of the functioning of the group. But, again, one should look first and develop one's categories later.

The environment of a group. As already defined, the environment of a group includes everything that is outside the boundary of a group. If we take as an example a group in which direct social work service is given to clients, the environment of such a group would include other groups in the agency, the agency as a whole, and the social worker who is working with the group. It would include other persons, clients and non-clients, who are related in significant ways to any of the members. And, of course, it would include all aspects of the larger community within which the group and the agency are found. While, from a theoretical point of view, the environment of the group must be conceived as including everything external to the group, for practical purposes it may be more useful, if one is trying to understand the group's present behaviour, to limit the enivironment to everything affecting the group in a significant way, *from its point of view.*

While, from a social work point of view, it may be more accurate to perceive the social worker as external to the group, there will be times when the group acts "as if" the worker were a member, and the behaviour of the group will have to be perceived accordingly in order to be fully understood. In fact, we return again to the important general principle that in order to understand the behaviour of any human organization, it is necessary to perceive the situation as the organism itself perceives it.

Parameters of a group's environment. Here will be included all those factors in the environment which are affecting the system or its sub-systems in any significant way. As in the case of the system variables, most will affect all of the sub-systems to some extent. For instance, the degree and manner in which the roles of men and women are delineated by the enveloping culture might be taken as an example of such an environmental parameter. Suppose that for a given group the statuses which men and women may occupy and the roles they may perform are rather rigidly and sharply differentiated. Suppose, further, that presiding over meetings is seen as exclusively a male function. Such activity, then, could not properly be a part of the executive system of a female group. Female groups would have to develop alternate ways of exercising the executive function. The assumption is made here, of course, that an "executive system" would prove to be one of the essential sub-systems of any group.

Group pathology. We know from experience that groups, like individuals, may become pathological, but in what sense may one speak of *group* pathology? What is the basis or locus of pathological conditions in groups? It seems likely that in every case a pathological condition may be traced to the malfunctioning of one or more of the functional sub-systems of the group. One or another of the sub-systems is not performing its normal function. If the disturbance in the sub-systems is sufficient to cause the group to depart from its steady state by a certain critical amount representing the tolerance of that group, then it can be regarded as being in a pathological condition. The malfunctioning of the system, likewise, might derive from the disruptive effects of one or more of the variables or environmental parameters of the system. Thus, to rectify the malfunctioning of a sub-system, it will usually be necessary to manipulate in some way the offending variables or parameters.

The group has been taken as an example to show how it may be represented as an organismic system. In a more complete formulation it would be necessary, and indeed possible, to represent the nature and functioning of individuals, organizations, and communities in a similar fashion.

PROSPECTS FOR A GENERIC THEORY OF PRACTICE

One reason why "system" was adopted as the central construct was that it seemed to hold prospect of providing the basis upon which a generic theory of practice might be built. If there are principles which apply to organismic systems in general, and if individuals, groups, organizations, and communities may be regarded as such systems, then these principles collectively might find their place in a unified theory of practice. They would provide a *common* framework for conceiving the individuals, groups, organizations, and communities as "clients," or as the means by which service is rendered to "clients." And all of this, in turn, would presumably increase the ultimate possibility of replacing current conceptions expressed in terms of the casework, group work, and community organization processes with what would be a generic and a more universally applicable *social work* process.

Let us pursue this possibility further to see whether our confidence in the utility of the construct "system" is likely to be justified. Is it possible to state certain propositions, derived from systems theory, which may be demonstrated by experience and ultimately by experiment, to apply equally well to the functioning of individuals, groups, organizations, and communities?

Encouraging progress toward this end is reported by the general systems theorists. Miller indicates that they have formulated several dozen specific theorems or propositions, each empirically testable at the levels of cell, organ, individual, small group, and society—often for the exchange of both energy and information—and that they have related these to their general theoretical framework.[10] Of those which Miller discusses in his article, certain ones in particular seem particularly relevant to a theory of social work practice and indicate the kind of formulations they are able to derive from their model.

One proposition holds that "living systems respond to continuously increasing stress first by a lag in response, then by an over-compensatory response, and finally by catastrophic collapse of the system."[11] Miller, in his elaboration of this proposition, reports that Selye's data from investigations of the effects of varying degrees of physiological stress on an organism[12] assume an order of which the curve illustrated in the diagram of Figure 5 is representative.

Initially, there is a dip in the curve in the direction of the final collapse, which

---

[10] Miller, "Toward a General Theory," p. 525.
[11] *Ibid.*, p. 527.
[12] H. Selye, *The Physiology and Pathology of Exposure to Stress; A Treatise Based on the Concepts of the General-Adaptation Syndrome and the Diseases of Adaptation* (Montreal: Acta, 1950).

is the alarm reaction. It is followed by a rise of the curve above the level
normally maintained by the organism, constituting a kind of over-compensation
or over-defensiveness. As stress is increased, more and more defences are called

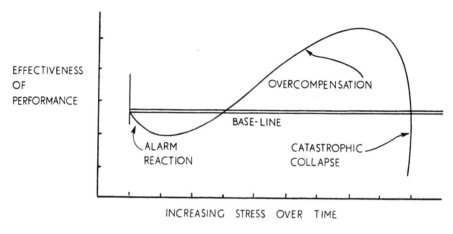

EFFECTIVENESS
OF
PERFORMANCE

OVERCOMPENSATION

BASE-LINE

ALARM
REACTION

CATASTROPHIC
COLLAPSE

INCREASING STRESS OVER TIME

FIGURE 5

into play until finally no additional ones are available and the system suddenly
collapses. How very familiar this process must sound to any social worker,
who must witness parts at least of this process almost daily in practice. What
may be surprising is the indication that the process is manifested also by all
lower orders of living organisms.

Two other propositions, stated in the language of general systems theory, also
describe phenomena which are frequently observed in social work. One is to
the effect that "there is always a constant systematic distortion—or better alter-
ation—between input of energy or information into a system and output from
that system." [13] The other suggests its source when it states that "the distortion of a system is the sum of the effects of processes which subtract from
the input to reduce strains in sub-systems or add to the output to reduce such
strains." [14] The phenomenon of distortion, to which the first of these propositions
refers, has many manifestations in the experience of the social worker. Workers
know how understanding and communication between themselves and the client
may be impaired by such distortion and how difficult it is to make the necessary allowances and the correct assumptions. The second of the two propositions
seems to provide a plausible and useful explanation of the cause of distortion.
In suggesting what happens to energy and information within the system to
lead to distortion, the proposition probably contributes to a greater understanding of, and even to the possibility of predicting, the form and direction
which the distortion may take.

In the experience of community organization there is abundant evidence
of the phenomenon to which another of Miller's propositions refers. It holds
that "when a system's negative feedback discontinues, its steady state vanishes,

[13]   Miller, "Toward a General Theory," p. 526.
[14]   *Ibid.,* p. 527.

and at the same time its boundary disappears and the system terminates." [15] This is an apt description of a committee which, when dealing with a practical problem, cannot agree. It may finally dissolve, the members dispersing while the larger organizational unit, which set up the committee, takes over the responsibility for settling the issue.

One further example described by Miller in a recent conversation with the author would seem to have very great relevance for social work practice. It is a proposition which holds that as the input of energy or information is increased, an organism reacts in a certain characteristic way. At first the organism is able to cope with the increasing input, but at a particular point it is unable to do so and experiences an "input overload." When this happens the organism tries to cope with the situation in one of three ways. (1) It may attempt to arrange the input in order and deal with one item at a time; (2) it may try to close itself, that is, stop additional input or (3) if the first two fail, the system may break down. The Mental Health Research Institute in its current research programme is finding support for this proposition in relation to every level of organism it has studied, and these include individuals, groups, and organizations.

We said that such a proposition is particularly pertinent to the theory of social work. It would seem so if we accept, as indeed we do, the idea that service is rendered to clients who are experiencing or may experience the disequilibrating effects of stressful situations. For, certainly, input overload, to which the proposition refers, would seem to be a common cause of stress. Could it be that as we learn more about how organisms of all kinds react to such conditions as input overload we might also learn more about those social work clients whose problems may result from such conditions? We believe so; indeed, this example and the others are the principal reason for our present enthusiasm and our continued interest in the utilization of general systems theory in social work. As well as providing a framework within which to develop a generic theory of social work practice, it seems to provide a means of tapping the vast reservoir of pertinent knowledge in the various physical and non-physical sciences for use in the extension of practice theory in the service professions.

REPRESENTATION OF THE CONTEXT OF SOCIAL WORK PRACTICE

It seems possible, also, to represent every situation in which a worker renders service as work in and with a system. While such representation may add little that is new at this stage, ultimately the conception of social work in such terms may considerably deepen the worker's understanding and increase the skill with which he works.

Every relationship in professional social work involves work with individuals, in groups, in organizations, and in communities. The worker is concerned with this total complex at all times although his immediate concern may be with a particular part of the total complex. Usually the total activity of any social worker will involve some direct experience with all four categories of human

[15] *Ibid.*, p. 529.

organization. At any given moment, whether he be working with an individual, a group, an organization, or a community, he is doing so in one or more of several status-roles. At all times he has the status and performs the general role of social worker. But beyond this he may occupy alternately the position and perform the roles of agent, consultant, teacher, leader, or member. As *agent* he acts as the extension of the agency and gives the kind of direct service to clients which, in terms of its function, it is the responsibility of the agency to provide. As *consultant* he is one whose opinions and reactions other workers seek in order to increase their own understanding and skill. As *teacher* he facilitates the processes by which workers accumulate, integrate, and internalize knowledge, develop attitudes which are consistent with a well-articulated personal philosophy of social work, and develop and refine their skill. As *leader* he carries administrative responsibility for executing some phase of the agency's programme. And as *member* he is related in some degree to other persons for purposes of social welfare but is not, at that moment, performing the roles of agent, consultant, teacher, or leader.

If we were to examine more closely the relationship implied by each of these status-roles, we would probably find that the worker interacts with or in the system in a somewhat different way and for a somewhat different purpose. Leader and member imply a position within the system whereas agent, consultant, and teacher suggest a position external to it. Serving as an agent is, partly at least, a process of manipulating environmental parameters or of making energy and information from the environment available to the system, consultation is a means by which the system objectifies experience in order to achieve and maintain an appropriate steady state; and teaching, in part at least, is a process of making information available to the system.

In the activity in which a worker is engaged at a given moment, it is always possible to define the *ultimate client*. For example, a worker may be talking with a prospective employer of one of his parolees. In this case the parolee is the ultimate client and as such may be regarded as a system whose maintenance in steady state the worker is trying to promote. In each situation there is also an *immediate object* of the relationship which may or may not be the ultimate client. The prospective employer, for instance, is the immediate object of the relationship but not the ultimate client. It may be more appropriate to regard him as part of the environment which the worker is manipulating on behalf of his client. Finally, it is possible in each instance to locate the worker. He may be a part of the distal or proximal environment, or he may be a part of a functioning system. Actually, the worker and the client, and even the agency, might all define his position differently. Thus, in a given situation, the agency might place the worker in the client's proximal environment, the worker perceive himself as being in the distal environment, whereas the client would be operating as if he and the worker were a functioning system.

Representation of the Process of Social Work

While this formulation has not purported to deal specifically with the social work process, it seems to be possible, nevertheless, to describe the process rather generally in terms of general systems theory, granting of course that a more comprehensive and intensive analysis would require the use of many other concepts within the systems construct. What, in general, does the worker do when he works with a system; what does the system do with what the worker does; and what happens as a result? To the extent to which these questions can be answered, the social work process can be linked to the concept "system" and provide the framework for a comprehensive theory of the helping process.

In general, the worker does two things, both of which are designed to enable the system to establish and maintain a steady state around that condition which represents the best possible relationship between the system and its environment. He assists in the modification of the parameters of the environment and in the modification of the variables within the system. Both are accomplished, of course, through many methods. There may be attempts to modify the effect of certain parameters of the environment. There may be attempts to bring more parameters of the environment to the awareness of the system, that is, to bring certain aspects from the distal into the proximal environment so that they begin to influence the behaviour of the system. There may be an attempt to do the reverse, that is, to remove some to the distal environment. There may be attempts to make the energy and informational resources of the environment more readily available for use in the system.

With respect to the system itself, the worker, similarly, may assist in many things. He may help the system develop the kind of structure best suited to the purposes for which it exists. If those purposes change, he will help the system change its structure accordingly. He will be concerned, as well, with the sub-systems of the system. Are they adequately developed? Are they functioning well both individually and collectively?

When working with an individual, the worker is dealing with a single human system, for everything else is a part of the individual's environment. When working with a group, however, he is working simultaneously with the group, as a system, and all the members, as individual systems. In this sense, the process is considerably more complicated. And work with organizations or with communities, likewise, adds other levels to the complex. Thus as one works successively with individuals, groups, organizations, and communities, the "client" becomes progressively more complex. In another sense, however, work with lower levels in the hierarchy of human systems may be more complicated, for one is likely to be involved with the system at a deeper level and will likely be helping it to cope with more complex problems.

The social work process is not represented alone, however, by what the worker does. It includes as well both the response of the system to what the worker does and what the system does on its own behalf. As a matter of fact, changes are occurring continuously within the system toward the maintenance of a steady state, regardless of the efforts of the social worker. The worker's efforts, at best, serve to facilitate and accelerate this natural process.

It has been suggested that a more complete formulation of the social work process would require the utilization of other concepts. For instance, it might very well be represented as a decision-making process. One might represent what the worker and the system do as actions resulting from a succession of decisions. A construct, therefore, with which to conceptualize the decision-making process might be of great value in social work theory, suggesting that "information theory," which concerns itself with the decision-making process, might consequently have considerable relevance and utility.

IMPLICATIONS FOR SOCIAL WORK EDUCATION

General systems theory, in addition to its utility in the representation of the social work process, may be particularly useful as a framework within which to conceive and analyse the processes of social work education. Social work education is responsible for seeing that students acquire the knowledge, attitudes, and skills essential to the professional practice of social work. An analysis based upon the systems construct would seem to support the following observations, among others that could be cited, concerning how best the profession might fulfil this aspect of its total responsibility.

The process of acquiring the necessary knowledge, attitudes, and skills is not confined to the one or two years of formal professional education. It begins before and continues, to some extent, as long as the worker practises. The knowledge, attitudes, and skills with which the worker emerges from professional education are not determined entirely by what the educators "put into him" as a system. They are determined, finally, by what the student as a system "takes out" of the experience. Consistent with the principle of equifinality, different initial conditions may lead to a similar final condition, and according to the principle of individual differences, similar inputs may lead to dissimilar final states. There are three implications in these principles for the development of curricula. First, students will likely emerge with different knowledge, attitudes, and skills from the same curriculum. Second, in order that the curriculum may serve the varying needs of students, it should afford each a broad range of choice. And third, in order to predict with greater precision the knowledge, attitudes, and skills with which the student will emerge, we need to learn much more than is at present known about what the student, as a system, does with the experiences and materials which he encounters in professional education.

The question is often asked, from which does the student profit more, from exposure to a single theory of personality or exposure to several contrasting theories? Whenever an instructor presents theory in the classroom, he is providing the student, as a system, with coded information which the latter may or may not choose to use. On one hand, it would seem that the richer the variety of information available, and thus the greater number of theories presented, the more useful it would be to the student. On the other hand, the system may have a maximum tolerance for diversity which the presentation of contrasting theories might exceed. Whether this is so and how the system responds to a massive bombardment of diverse information is something about which we seem to know relatively little. It may be that most students have a greater capacity for handling a massive bombardment than they are usually assumed to possess and that educators should be less concerned with limiting volume and diversity in the curriculum and more concerned with developing skill in detecting when the tolerance level of the individual student has been exceeded.

This same phenomenon might be viewed in terms of input overload. The system can absorb a greater and greater input of energy and information up to the point of input overload when the system either succeeds in restricting further input or it becomes immobilized. Again, in social work education we should be striving to learn our students' tolerance levels and aiming to reach their maximum input tolerance without exceeding it.

Finally, with respect to social work education, a comment seems indicated concerning the continued use of the traditional division of social work into social casework, social group work, and community organization. The implication here seems quite obvious. In terms of general systems theory, continued use of these artificial divisions simply has no justification. Only one process is involved and that is the social work process. The continued use of these traditional divisions seems to imply that the three processes are governed by different principles, a suggestion which is inconsistent with general systems theory. Furthermore, continued use of this system of classification, while not directly implying so, does seem to suggest that social workers use one or other of these processes to the exclusion of the others. This, in practice, is seldom, if ever, the case. Every social worker, to some extent, works with individuals, groups, organizations, and communities. If one chooses to operate within the framework of general systems theory, the implications for social work education seem obvious. One would have to operate on the premise that we are educating *social workers,* not group workers, caseworkers, or community organization workers; and we are preparing them to perform the many tasks of the social worker. It would follow, too, of course, that we would desist from continued reference to ourselves as group workers, caseworkers, or community organization workers and our agencies as casework, group work, and community organization agencies. More and more we would think of ourselves as social workers and our agencies as agencies for social welfare.

PROGRAMME FOR THE FUTURE

Most of what has been claimed in this final chapter, necessarily and admittedly, has been conjectural. Certainly, a very great deal remains to be done before the tangible contributions of general systems theory toward the illumination and refinement of social work practice are clearly demonstrated. In general there are three tasks to be undertaken. The first, obviously, is an objective study of the human realities with which we are dealing in social work practice. The second is model building—the development of models capable of conceptualizing these human realities. And the third is the testing of the validity and utility of our models by determining whether their application leads to new insights for practice and ultimately to the rendering of better service.

I. The Study of Objective Realities in the Domain of Social Work

This part of the task might be undertaken as a rather extensive project involving the following sequence of steps. First, those items of the literature of social work practice most extensively used in social work education would be selected for analysis. Second, these items would be analysed to differentiate three kinds of statements: (*a*) statements of value, (*b*) statements of natural fact about the physical and non-physical world, and (*c*) principles or guides to action for the worker in relating to his world of reality.[16] This would be the basic task which, once accomplished, would permit the undertaking of a number of other projects:

1. Statements of value could be examined to determine the nature and the range of philosophical positions represented in the educational preparation of social workers. The results of this survey could be compared with those items in the literature which have attempted to state the philosophy of social work.

2. Statements of fact concerning the nature of human organization, in its various forms, could be examined. One could examine statements in social work literature about individuals, groups, organizations, and communities, distinguishing those facts which are generic to all from those which are specific to each. By such a means one would determine, on one hand, the properties which are assumed to be common, and on the other, the properties which are unique to individuals, groups, organizations, and communities. In this connection and as a second phase of the project one might examine the various generic propositions being enunciated by the general systems theorists to determine the extent to which they coincide with or might be incorporated into those now in social work literature.

3. Statements defining the principles of social work practice could also be examined to determine which are common and which are specific to casework, group work, and community organization. Presumably, out of such an analysis a conception of the social work process would eventually develop.

It should be recognized that all the projects described above assume the validity and accuracy of the statements of value, fact, and principle contained in current social work literature. Since such statements should never actually be assumed to be completely valid, any and all studies which tested their validity would make an important contribution to this phase of the undertaking.

II. Model Building

The function and necessity of models in theory building has been fully elaborated in Part I of this monograph. A number of specific projects related to model building for social work theory could and should be undertaken.

1. Assuming, for reasons already stated, that the organismic model is the most appropriate for the over-all conceptualization of human organization in its various forms, it would seem desirable to undertake a further explication of this particular model. One way in which this might be accomplished would be to explore the literature of the behavioural sciences to determine the extent

---

[16] The author is indebted to Ernest Greenwood for this suggestion.

and ways in which the organismic model has been used. Presumably this exploration ought to include its application to all types of living matter with special attention to its use in the case of individuals, groups, organizations, and communities. Such a survey would make it possible to develop a much more precise and detailed description of the organismic model.

2. A separate project, although one which obviously would be closely related to the above, would be a survey of the behavioural propositions considered to be generic to organismic systems at all levels, a survey which should include, as well, a continuing review of whatever research is undertaken to test the validity and generality of these propositions.

3. The first two proposals would necessarily involve the more macroscopic view of the organism. In addition to these, an almost endless number of microscopic studies could be undertaken. These would be studies of certain aspects or sub-systems of the organism. One such study might be an exploration and classification of the various feedback mechanisms to be found in human organismic systems. The study by Virginia Carlson, a member of the 1957 Berkeley research group, has already made a valuable contribution to this area of analysis. It will be recalled (cf. p. 46) that she employed the feedback concept in her analysis of the dynamics of a riot situation in a correctional institution, and indicated among other things that there are a great many different kinds of feedback mechanisms.

4. Another type of microscopic study might be an examination of the phenomena of openness and closedness in organismic systems. Here a great many questions could be explored. How does the organism achieve openness and closedness? How may the relative degrees of openness and closedness in a system be measured? How may one assess the optimum balance between openness and closedness for any system under any particular set of circumstances? This question of openness and closedness seems to be of crucial importance at all levels of human organization. It has been suggested that one of the great issues of our time is to determine what is, and how to obtain, the proper balance between security (closedness) and freedom (openness). There are times when a nation, fearful for its security, closes its boundaries to "foreign" influences; there are other times when the nation, fearful of encroachments upon individual freedoms, opens its boundaries. McCarthyism is perhaps a familiar example of the former, the recent decisions of the United States Supreme Court concerning the rights of the individual, of the latter. Alternately, groups seem to act to exclude those members who deviate in certain ways from the majority and at other times seek to incorporate new members who will bring "new blood" into the organization. Individuals, likewise, seem to seek the security which derives from the orderliness and conformity associated with closedness, but at other times seek the freedom and stimulation which derive from openness.

The same phenomenon is manifest in a profession and in professional education. Professions establish boundaries determining who may, or may not, enter and they establish standards and policies concerning what are appropriate attitudes, knowledge, and skills for their members. In so doing they promote the closedness of the system. At the same time, the profession encourages and rewards experimentation and creativity and in so doing promotes openness. So it is with professional education. Accreditation of professional schools tends to promote closedness and all its attendant consequences while the autonomy granted by the profession, and the freedom insured by the membership of a school in an independent institution of higher learning, contribute to the maintenance of openness. There are perhaps few other aspects of organismic systems that refer to more phases of the social work profession than this phenomenon of openness-closedness, and certainly it would be a most interesting realm of inquiry.

5. Finally, there is another major project in model building—major in both extent and importance. It is the task of specifying for individuals, groups, organizations, and communities what are their essential functional sub-systems. Again much work has already been done in the behavioural sciences and anyone wishing to enter this domain ought to undertake a thorough survey of the literature to examine the typologies that already have been proposed.

III. Reality Testing and Utilization of the Model

The third group of projects has to do with testing and using the model. Such projects would explore two questions: (1) Can the phenomena we encounter in the real world be described in terms of our model? And (2) if they can, do such descriptions provide new insights for practice?

1. Once the organismic model has been developed to the tentative satisfaction of the theorist, it should be used to describe a variety of social work clients—and here, as Lippitt, Watson, and Westley have done, we contend that groups, organizations, and communities, as well as individuals, may be regarded as clients as well as the means of helping clients. Several members of the 1957 Berkeley research group have made important contributions to this part of the task. Helen Perroti and Roberta Solbrig, using the organismic model, have described individual clients with whom they have worked, and the latter has reported, with her supervisor's corroboration, that her analysis in such terms led to new insight and to substantial movement in the case. Ann Tompkins described a group with which she had been working in terms of the same model. The study by Herbst, referred to earlier in this chapter, is another example of the use of the model in relation to a group. These few instances are insufficient, of course, to provide conclusive answers to the question of the universal applicability or utility of the model, but they do lend sufficient support to warrant further applications.

2. The organismic model can and should be used for purposes of analysing the structure and functioning of social work agencies. As already reported, Virginia Carlson, in her description of a correctional institution, has successfully and fruitfully applied the model.

3. There is a good deal of evidence to suggest that when a social worker deals with a case, although his primary client may be an individual, he is in fact dealing with an involved complex consisting of his client, among other individuals—in groups—in a community. Someone should try to represent this complex as an organismic system—as the system, in fact, which the social worker in the final analysis is trying to help maintain itself in a steady state. This task alone

would help us to move a long way towards a generic conception of the social work process.

4. It seems possible, too, that the social work profession may be regarded as an organismic system. Henrietta Gillenwater, another member of the 1957 Berkeley research group, has undertaken such a task and has been able to sketch its structure in systemic terms and to suggest what may be the functional subsystems of the social work profession. This project should continue in view of her encouraging beginning. Social work, we must remember, is a comparatively young profession still in its formative stages and engaged at present in the development of a single professional organization out of a number of related but separate professional entities. Considerable profit might accrue if this task, envisaged and pursued within the framework of the organismic model, were to be continued.

5. Of course, in the longer view of the project, there is the social work process itself, although, in this formulation, it has not been a principal point of focus. Once progress has been made toward describing the client in systemic terms, it ought to be possible to suggest how the worker functions in relation to client systems and to describe the social work relationship and the total social work process in systemic terms. This, of course, is the ultimate objective towards which this whole research programme is directed.

A FINAL WORD

The superiority of programmatic research over a procedure that proliferates a series of independent and unco-ordinated research projects has been amply demonstrated in every field, although in social work it is only in recent years that research has, in many instances, taken the programmatic form. The hope that the present project might provide a possible framework for a comprehensive and systematic research *programme* has been, in fact, one of the chief reasons why it was undertaken.

The development of theory which will serve to increase understanding and improve service is an objective to which all professional social workers can subscribe. Its fullest accomplishment, however, requires the contribution of every member of the profession—the contribution of which each is capable by virtue of his particular interests and talents. Because theory building has so many facets, there is a myriad of ways in which every practitioner and theorist may and should participate. If the present project has served to stimulate any greater interest and commitment to the theory building aspect of professional responsibility, if it has suggested any point at which one might begin to exercise that responsibility, it will have served a very useful purpose and achieved the principal end to which it was directed.

INDEX

INDEX

AGING PROCESS, 45
Allport, F. H., 7, 12, 39, 44, 47, 55, 56
Allport, G. W., 57
analogues, definition of, 11
Aptekar, H. H., 23

BECOMING, process of, 57
Berkeley Research Group, vi, viii, 33
Bertalanffy, L. von, 39, 41, 44, 45, 46, 48, 49
Beshers, J. M., 10
Bisno, H., 29
boundary, definition of, 42
Bray, H. G., 44, 45, 46
Burton, A. C., 50

CARLSON, V., 46, 47, 75, 76
Carnot, N. L. S., 34
Carter, G., 16, 25, 61
Cervinka, V., 63
circuits, self-closing, 7
community organization, 73
Conant, J. B., 2, 3, 8, 23
concept, definition of, 9
conceptualizing, definition of, 11
concretizing, definition of, 17
construct, definition of, 10
construct "system," justification of choice of, 52-3
constructual framework, definition of, 11
Coyle, G. L., 20

DIMOCK, H. S., 61

EATON, J. W., 40, 54, 57
energy, 65
entropy: definition of, 34; positive, 41, 45; negative, 34, 45
environment: definition of, 42
equifinality: definition of, 44-5; principle of, 72
equilibrium, 41
Erikson, E., 16, 57
event-structures, 56

FAGEN, R. E., 39, 47
functional unity, 46
feedback, 75; amplification, 47; control mechanism, relay, 48, continuous, 48, intermittent, 47, proportional, 48; dampened, 48; definition of, 46; mainline function to, 47; negative, 47; positive, 47; processes, 46-8

Fromm, E., 34

GENERAL SYSTEMS THEORY, 38-9

Generic Theory of Practice, prospects for, 67-9
George, F. H., 11
Gillenwater, H., 77
Greenwood, E., 2, 17, 22, 23, 24, 25, 74
Grinker, R. R., 40
group: boundary of, 64; environment of, 66, parameters of, 66; existence of, 63-4; functioning of, 64-5; pathology, 66-7; structure of, 64; system, parameters of as a, 65-6, as an organismic, 63-7
groupoid, definition of, 63-4

HALL, A. D., 39, 47
Hearn, G., vi, 42
Henderson, L. J., 39
Herbst, P. G., 63, 76
Hill, W. F., 64
Hoffman, I. L., 19, 20, 21, 22, 25
Hoyle, F., 34
human beings, characteristics of, 43
human nature, 34-5
human systems, choice of model for, 42-4
hypothesis, definition of, 9

INFORMATION, 65
information theory, 72
input overload, 69, 73
inputs and outputs, 44

JOULE, J. P., 34

KAHN, A. J., 20
Kelvin, W. T., 34
Klein, A. F., 4
Kluckhohn, C., 35
knowing: non-scientific, 26; possibilities of, 32-3; scientific, 26; definition of, 1
knowing process, 5
  elements in, 1-5; communication, definition of, 5; conceptualizing, definition of, 3; concretizing, definition of, 4, 17; experiencing, definition of, 2; testing, definition of, 4; well-ordered empirical inquiry, definition of, 2;
  as a functional unity, 5-7
Köhler, W., 44
Kotinsky, R., 16

LEWIN, K., 7, 9, 59
life in the universe, nature of, 33-5

www.ingramcontent.com/pod-product-compliance
Ingram Content Group UK Ltd.
Pitfield, Milton Keynes, MK11 3LW, UK
UKHW050444010225
454513UK00007B/248

9 781487 591533